Spirit Associates

Spirit Associates

Your user-friendly guide to spirit guides, allies, and teachers.

Bill Duvendack

Stafford, England

Spirit Associates by Bill Duvendack

Cover Art: Danielle Lainton
Editor: Danielle Lainton
Layout: Danielle Lainton

Set in Book Antiqua

MB0212
ISBN: 978-1-912241-20-0

A Megalithica Books Publication
http://www.immanion-press.com
info@immanion-press.com

Contents

Dedication

This book is dedicated to all beings of light, everywhere.

Introduction

Spirit guides are a subject that has been extensively written about, especially over the last ten years or so, but having been working with them for a lot longer than that, I feel this book is appropriate to clean up some misconceptions and complete other lines of thought that have been left undone. I immediately state this because I am fully aware of the multitude of spirit guide books out there, and I know many may be looking at this book and asking themselves "Why another book on spirit guides?"

However, this book is built on the foundation that has already been established in this series, "Vocal Magick," Spirit Relations," and "Psychic Protection." Yes, you can read this one without having read the others, but I will constantly be referencing things from those books. "Spirit Associates" will connect heavily with "Spirit Relations," and the easy way to think of this connection is that "Spirit Relations" gave you the skills, and now it is time to put them to work for you when it comes to interacting with spirits. Because there are so many different kinds of spirits, we will start with the immediate ones around us, so we will not be discussing angels or demons or gods or goddesses, or anything of that nature. I will touch on this later in the book, but this work will specifically focus on our immediate family. Or, if you prefer, our immediate spirit associates.

Technically, believing in the existence of spirit guides and what I will discuss here is still considered a belief (and therefore completely subjective), rather than a fact. But I know a lot of people that have had encounters with their spirit allies that have been more tangible and real than paying monthly bills. Yes, I see their existences as facts because I am one of those people. I have had many intense, vivid experiences with spirit guides over the years that have convinced me of their existence, but I respect those that don't believe in them, a point I will discuss later.

This information is meant as a framework, which means you should feel free to modify the parts that work as you see fit to align with your spiritual paradigm. This could mean changing titles on some of these subjects, or throwing some out while changing the names and titles of others. As I will share later, I have adjusted some things, myself. This is the perk of the subjective nature of this material. It can be individually adapted. There is something to keeping to the integrity of this structure though, as you bring yourself into further alignment with the tradition and therefore, the egregore, but there is a lot of room for personal nuances and variances as you will see. It is up to you to find the balance when it comes to aligning with this integrity vs personal adaptation.

In a lot of ways, what we will be talking about here is a form of spiritual technology, a subject which requires its own book. Spiritual technology is when you have a spiritual system that is true, regardless of spiritual and religious veneers. Hindu mantras come to mind, as well as the Enochian magical system, and sacred body postures, known under different names in different cultures. There are many other examples out there, and you may find value in looking them up. They really open your mind when you ponder them, and even more so when you learn them. This is the perspective I have on spirit guides, and the reason this matters is because it drives home the point that what we're discussing here is something that can be grafted onto almost any other belief system out there. I realize this is not in line with traditional Spiritualism, but we're in the 21st century, not the 19th, when it started. To paraphrase Charles Darwin, it is the most adaptable that survives, and currently there are a lot of adaptations happening when it comes to spiritual beliefs and religions.

In chapter one we will address this topic more in-depth, but I offer it up here in the introduction because spiritual technology can be found and used anywhere, and therefore it is greater than this book, but the knowledge of it is a key to unlock a large part of this book. Practically, all of this means that I see spirit guides in a more spiritual light, doing my best to be unrestrained from dogma of any one particular religion or belief system.

I am biased, though, as I was an ordained Spiritualist minister for nine years, which occurred after a three-year seminary program, which was after about a year or twos' worth of formal classes. My journey with Spiritualism began in 2006, so yes, I do have bias. This was not traditional Spiritualism, though. At the time, it was the cutting edge of the independent Spiritualist movement. This may seem like a detail, but you will see how large it plays out later when it comes to understanding and working with spirit associates. Understand that I am aware of my bias, and I do my best to confront it and keep its influence to a minimum. There will be a book in the future that will discuss independent Spiritualism that I will write, so for now I tease you with that, just to make sure you chuckle, as we dive into the world of our spirit associates. Cheers!

Bill Duvendack
Sirius Rising, 2021

Chapter One: Spiritualism, the Necessary Pieces

While the concept and title of spirit guides is a fairly recent invention, essentially, they have been around for a long time. It is only recently that things have become structured and codified in such a way that it is digestible for everyone. In almost, if not all world religions and spiritual traditions, non-physical spirits are addressed. While titles, powers, and relationships to them may vary from place to place there are some overall themes. One of those themes is that humans can connect with these spirits and work with them on an ongoing basis, establishing long-lasting relationships that are beneficial to all involved. This is important to keep in mind because in some ways it tells us that the more things change, the more they stay the same.

Since almost the beginning of time, people have communicated with the spiritual world. This can be found in many different belief systems across the world, and spiritual literature is rife with stories of how this communication radically altered some sort of the past. The first character that comes to mind was the Oracle at Delphi, but technically Moses speaking to the burning bush is one as well. Usually, the results of these conversations have led to major acts of good or evil on the part of the human, but what about the thousands that happen every day, both then and now? Yes, those are valid spirit interactions, too, but they are generally not as profound regarding global or species impact.

Spiritualism, a Brief History

Spirit guides as we understand them today come from the American religion of Spiritualism, which began on March

31, 1848 in Hydesville New York. While this religion started in the USA, it quickly spread out into the global world, and with the development of the World Wide Web, has spread even further into nations and societies that may not fully accept it from a physical world perspective. In this way it has evolved far beyond its humble and very focused roots. We will come back to this point later, but it does need mentioned here, because the religion of Spiritualism is a dynamic and modern example of how religions change over time and exposure to new ideas and places.

Spiritualism began with the spirit wrappings of the Fox sisters. I will skip a lot of the details, because they have been covered by authors greater than I (Such as Sir Arthur Conan Doyle), but some background is necessary for context to move forward later. I will summarize the story here.

Like many religions, the true origins are shrouded in mystery. First, the facts. The two youngest Fox sisters, Leah and Margaretta, developed a system of spirit wrappings to convince their older sister, Catherine, that they were hearing spirits. All three were living in a house in Hydesville NY with their parents. The house was supposedly haunted, and in late March of 1848, they experienced unexplained sounds coming from inside. Leah and Margaretta, established a system of communication (the aforementioned spirit wrappings) with a spirit whom they named "Mr Splitfoot." Through questions, answers, and experiments, they established a rapport with the spirit, who claimed his name was Charles Rosna. Of course this created quite the stir, and not only was the family involved in the spirit communication, neighbors were, too. Mr Rosna told the story that he was murdered there five years earlier and buried in the cellar. This was somewhat validated by neighbors who did report that they believed there was someone murdered there before the Fox family occupied it.

I am pretty sure you can see where this is going. The cellar was dug up, and some shards of bone were found, thus validating the spirit. However, a missing person named Charles Rosna was never confirmed. While this may sound suspicious, keep in mind that this was 1848, so it is not *that* unlikely or odd. From here, the rest as they say, is history; the girls went on to get as good of an education as they could get, and became professional mediums, arguably the first ones in the USA. This was the seed that germinated into Spiritualism. In a lot of ways, the time was ripe for such a movement. The 1700s was the time of the Christian mysticism and enlightenment movement, and people such as Emanuel Swedenborg, Franz Mesmer, and Karl von Eckhartshausen, were all at the forefront of developing and expanding that movement. In a lot of ways, this was the first stage of metaphysics, too, which shows us how Spiritualism and metaphysics are intertwined.

Let's look at some context to understand how all of this developed. The Fox sisters first had their spirit wrappings in March of 1848, and thus their experiments and work would continue through that year and into 1849. Then, it would have taken time to develop. In 1861 the USA had the American Civil War, which lasted until 1865. This war is the war that claimed the most American lives of any war, and it was really quite horrific in a lot of ways. It divided family against family, and families within families. This means that a lot of people lost loved ones, and many times unexpectedly. This created a desire to know if there was life after death. This also created the desire to contact deceased loved ones, and with this new movement of Spiritualism, a path was given for those that wanted to explore and contact the other side. Because of this, Spiritualism saw a boom time.

A second perspective for context was that Spiritualism

was coming into being on the heels of the New Thought Movement, which came into being in the early 1800s. In a lot of ways, this was an extension and evolution of the Christian Mysticism movement, and took a more enlightened, liberal, expansive approach to all things spiritual. Beliefs such as 1) Infinite Intelligence/God is everywhere, 2) Divinity is found everywhere, 3) Love is the highest spiritual principle, and 4) Our minds are the greatest tools we have for manifestation. If you're reading this book, I am confident that you recognize a lot of these teachings from other various places.

It would be wise to also keep in mind that the Rosetta Stone's discovery had only recently happened, and a few years after Spiritualism came into being, certain baked clay tablets from the Mesopotamia area of the world were discovered and translated. Egypt was held by the UK at that time, so these two fields of study, ancient Egypt and Sumeria, were flourishing and popular. These both fueled the evolution of thought and provided ample material for the other organizations we are discussing to incorporate and stimulate.

Outside of the USA, and in some areas of it, the Western Esoteric Tradition was also going through its own boom time, especially in Europe and the rest of the Old World. A lot of the 1800s was motivated by the French Occult Revival, but also included the advent of Theosophy, an increase in Rosicrucianism, Freemasonry, and the eventual creation of the Hermetic Order of the Golden Dawn. This was not the only order to come out of this time, but it is the one that has had the greatest impact, historically speaking. When you put the two pieces together, you can see how much was occurring globally and locally during that century.

Decades after the American Civil War, Leah and Margaretta recanted their spirit rapping sessions, saying that they were hoaxes. Of course this led to diminishment of the legitimacy of Spiritualism and spirit contact in general, but there is still a lot of debate today as to whether their confessions were legitimate or coerced. There are many debates out there that say the only reason the younger girls recanted was because they were not only coerced to, but also that there were financial reasons involved in the picture. This is the mist of mystery - was it legitimate contact or a con job? Really, as is true with so many other religions, it really doesn't matter. If the system works, then it works, and there's no debating the semantics. Charlatans and frauds are unfortunately too common throughout the history of Spiritualism, so regardless of the veracity of the claims, it is a trait of the egregore. Spiritualism does teach ways to spot a fraud though, which means that the majority of people are aware of this trait and do their best to protect and encourage others to use critical thinking.

The next major boom time for Spiritualism came in the 1920s. This was due to the fact that World War I (1914-1918) had recently ended with a staggering death toll on all fronts. The same idea was held in the minds of many; people wanted to know if there was life after death, and they wanted to contacted deceased loved ones for various reasons. While these boom times were good for the development of Spiritualism, we can see that this was born from tragedy, something every well-trained medium can handle. A major problem with the boom times for Spiritualism is that the more popular something is, the easier it is to be used to defraud others. After the Roarin' Twenties, Spiritualism quieted down for a few years, until of course, World War II (1939-1945) happened.

After World War II, Spiritualism did get a boost, yes, but not as much as it had previously received. There are various reasons for this. One is that the charlatans were known about, so the credibility of Spiritualism was not what it was previously. Secondly, technology played a larger role. It was easier to communicate with others using the telephone, radio, telegraph, etc. This helped to hasten the spread of ideas, diminishing the role of Spiritualism, and really, religion in general. One of the ways this played out was in the sphere of occultism. Post-WW II brought more emphasis on the occult and modern spirituality in general, rather than just emphasizing one particular religion. Ceremonial magick, the new religion of Wicca, and the entrance into the Atomic Age, all underwent periods of expansion, so the post-war expansion was as not focused in one direction, but rather diffused and spread through many different venues.

Spiritualism did play a key role in overturning the Witchcraft Act laws in the United Kingdom, and in 1951, many of the sections of those laws were repealed. The Fraudulent Mediums Act of 1951 replaced much of the outdated code. This is worth noting because it shows the interconnectedness between Spiritualism and witchcraft. I know many Spiritualists that are not into witchcraft, and I know many witches that are not into Spiritualism, so this is not a strong connection, but between the political activism of spiritualists in the UK and the work of Gerald Gardner, the UK made a lot of progress in a few short years, and in a lot of ways, opened the door for more modern religions, such as Anton Lavey's Church of Satan and the religion of Satanism, another American product.

Because of the diversity of modern spiritual teachings after World War II, Spiritualism declined in popularity during the 1950s, but I should make it clear here that it was not so much a decline, as it was a lack of a boom time. From the outside it may look like a decline, but in reality, it was more of a quiet time as the religion developed behind the scenes, so to speak. The religion itself had been around for about one hundred years now, so it had gained traction and solidified, but now there were other alternative belief systems available to others. As is the case with many things that are shiny and new, they drew the eye of the casual seeker, and thus the cultural revolution of the 1960s occurred.

Most of what occurred during that time is still remembered by many living practitioners, and there are volumes in existence that go into great detail about that time period. The short version is that during that time, there was an expansion of all things occult and non-mainstream religious and spiritual. More emphasis and credence were given not only to occultism and its various branches, but also to faiths outside the norm of western society. Drugs and the power of music to bring people together was another product of that time, and because of all of this, a renewed interest was taken in subjects that had long been hidden or taboo. Even though in this chapter we have discussed the broad development of the Western Esoteric Tradition, it was only during the nineteen fifties and sixties that the scope of it all was magnified and cleaned up in a lot of ways. Spiritualism only profited from this by being exposed to more people, which allowed it to grow and prosper. Yes, it was still seen as a common breeding ground for frauds, but in comparison to other spiritual and religious systems, it could be argued that it was in the minority of skeptics.

From the 1960s until now, it has undergone growth and change, and has in some ways, split in two. Over the last sixty years, it has integrated itself with the Western Esoteric Tradition in various ways. Some of these ways have been at the direction of Spiritualism in general, while other ways have cropped up due to greater spiritual movements that were happening concurrently. For example, for much of the 1970s until now, Spiritualism has been deeply embedded with the "New Age" movement, or as I like to call it, the "Ancient Wisdom" movement. This has tied it in with Theosophy, channeled material, revealed teachings, and many other modern schools of thought.

Even though it is older than all of these, it has still found a home.

A major reason for this is what we will be discussing for the remainder of the chapter. Spiritualism stands alone as its own religion, but it exists in such a way that it can be grafted onto other spiritual systems to great effect, as you will see below. Traditional Spiritualism has to do with connecting the spirits of loved ones, but through the course of the last few decades, a focus has changed to include simply channeling techniques, specifically for the sake of connecting with one's own spirit guides and teachers. Functionally, this means that there are some Spiritualists out there that have probably never channeled a deceased family member of any kind, but rather spend the bulk of their time and energy working with their own personal spirit guides and other associates. This is how we arrive at where we are now. Traditional Spiritualism and Spiritualist churches still do commonly exist, but there has been an increase in the development and expansion of an "Independent Spiritualist" branch.

In a lot of ways, this has occurred with the rise in the number of people that are "spiritual but not religious." This is a human trait that has been increasing in frequency with the rise of the Ancient Wisdom movement, and the essence of it is simply: One focuses on their spiritual development rather than adhering to any one dogmatic faith. People that are this way claim that this makes them feel more comfortable in their own spiritual skin so to speak, and they are generally more relaxed and proactive when it comes to who they are and what they are learning about themselves during this lifetime. This also allows for a large degree of eclecticism, so that people of this mindset can tailor-make their spiritual path to what they feel is right. It is the Independent Spiritualist movement that I was trained in, but that church descended from traditional Spiritualism, so I have a heavy background in that, too. I offer this information here in the name of transparency.

Key Contributions of Spiritualism

Spiritualism has contributed much to modern spirituality in general, but specifically when it comes to updating many occult topics. The biggest gift it has given is the systematic study of spirits and specifically working with them. Remember that it was born during a time when a lot of scientific experimentation was occurring. This is reflected in Franz Mesmer's experiments as well as Benjamin Franklin's studies regarding electricity. Both of these, and several others, occurred before the creation of Spiritualism, but they definitely contributed to the budding metaphysical movement, which paved the way for Spiritualism. Phrenology, eugenics, and other scientific fields that have since been proven false were quite common at this time, and these serve to demonstrate that at that time, science was exploring and expanding. This covered more than just scientific sciences, as the scientific method of thinking was also being developed and expanded. Clarity of thought and the integration of logic and reason with emotions, was highly emphasized in spiritual writings.

If you want a good example of this, look at the fictitious character Sherlock Holmes. Sir Arthur Conan Doyle created the character, and it is worth noting that Doyle was a Spiritualist. As a matter of fact, one of the best, if not the best, books on the history of Spiritualism comes from his pen. Holmes' way of using deduction and paying attention to details gives us insight into how this spiritual renaissance was playing out at that time. Doyle was developing Holmes in the latter part of the nineteenth century, which was quite active from a modern spiritual perspective. The Hermetic Order of the Golden Dawn, The Theosophical Society, Rosicrucianism, Freemasonry, and many branches of Christianity (Such as Mormonism) were coming into being at this time, and poets such as Emerson and Thoreau were writing about related topics as well. In this way, it was an evolution of the use of the mind, as well as how we as a species view spirituality in general.

Let's turn our attention to the details, now that we have established the bigger picture. Spiritualism gave us mediumship tools to use. Tools used to contact spirits have been around for thousands of years before that, and are as diverse as humanity, but Spiritualism brought a lot of them together for people to learn about, and even added new ones to the repertoire. Let's walk through an example to clarify. Let's say that you were interested in Spiritualism at that time. It was new, so skepticism was quite common and understandable, but you decide to check it out. Not only do you get introduced to spirits and spirit contact, you also learn about various tools that you can use to contact spirits. And of course, with experience, training, and education, you can eventually make your own spirit contact tools!

In short, because Spiritualism is a religion, it provides a community for people of a like mind. For centuries before that, you might have been born and raised with a desire and natural affinity for contacting spirits, but the only tools you would have been exposed to in order to make this happen were the ones from your immediate family and the few friends that you knew (Remember, travel and communication were harder then than they are now). You might try those tools, have no success, and think that the problem was you, or something else that was probably a self-defeatist thought. Now, with Spiritualism, if one tool did not work for spirit contact, you could simply try a different tool, and you could continually go through this process until you found your rhythm and affinity. In its early years, Spiritualism traveled around quite a bit, so in this way it was kind of like a spiritual carnival. Yes, it was billed that way and done in that fashion, but this helped to spread all of these things to new areas that had never been exposed to anything like it.

Tools

The first tool to mention is a common one, the much-vaulted crystal ball. Seeing, also known as scrying, by staring into a reflective or clear surface, has been done in various global cultures for thousands of years. There are many ways to do this. The first is to use a crystal ball, egg, or some other form. You gaze into it and let your eyes unfocus. As you do so, you stimulate parts of your mind that are not otherwise stimulated, and you allow yourself to absorb the impressions you see in it. You can scry into almost anything, from a clear quartz crystal to a pool of water, as was commonly done in ancient cultures such as Greece and Egypt. I have scried in many different types of crystals over the years and have found that the visions and messages are tied into the type of stone and its correspondences. For example, when scrying into a citrine sphere, a lot of the images and messages were about prosperity, health, and good fortune.

Scrying has been present in occultism for centuries, but the common tool used there is the black mirror. Yes, there are many instances of scrying into crystals in grimoires and other writings, but the more common tool that was used was a mirror painted black, which could be effective in low light conditions. The mirror would either be painted with reflective black paint, or black glass would be used. This method heavily relies on low-light conditions, whereas with the crystal ball the lightning does not really matter, past the usual ritual role. An extension of this is to fill a chalice, cauldron, or some other similar, sacred container, with liquid, and scry in it.

A spirit board is the next tool we will discuss. Most

people reading this are familiar with the "Ouija" board, but keep in mind that it was released in 1891, almost fifty years after the beginning of Spiritualism, but we can see the influence of Spiritualism in its creation and patent. Like scrying devices though, spirit boards have been around a lot longer than the Ouija brand. Generally, a spirit board is made of a sacred wood. This may sound esoteric, but really all it means is that a wood with metaphysical properties that align with spirit work was used, so it was not a particular type of wood, but rather a wood that was chosen because of its characteristics. For example, cedar would be a good choice of wood to use because in many spiritual traditions, cedar is an excellent conduit and amplifier for spirit contact. The next time you think of your favorite cedar chest, you may want to keep that in mind! Once the wood was chosen and refined, the letters of the alphabet were put on it, as well as the list of basic numbers. Many times, words like "yes," "no," "maybe," or "goodbye" were also put on it. Since we're discussing wood here, you can also deduce that this information was burned into the wood or engraved there. Some spirit boards did not use letters of the alphabet at all, and instead used runes or other magical glyphs or symbols that could be used to convey messages through the finer planes.

One of my favorites is next on the discussion list, and that is the spirit trumpet. No, it is not a trumpet dedicated exclusively to spirit work, but rather it is more like a horn. On one end it has a narrow opening, and it flares out as a cone into a wider opening at the other end. Traditionally, there would be rings of paint or some other substance that can be easily seen in little to no light. When performing seances, the trumpet would be placed on the table in the spirit chamber, and during the session, it would rise or fall, depending on the activity of the spirit present. It is similar to a spirit board in that the material used to make it would be chosen for its metaphysical correspondences. For example, if someone was going to use it regularly and for a long time, it could be made of metal, because metal holds vibrations and energy longer than wood. You could then micromanage this further, to select a certain type of metal, and you could even go so far as to align this alchemically. Thus, if you wanted to achieve the highest possible energetics and vibrations using it, you could use tin, which is the metal of Jupiter, the planet of expansion and spirituality. I have used spirit trumpets while on spirit investigations at various places, and I used it differently than this. The way I used it was to treat it like an instrument that the spirit or spirits could use to contact me. So, I would hold it up to my ear and simply listen. These sessions were quite profound, but yes, it was not a traditional application of the trumpet.

A curious tool, and one that was used widely fraudulently, was that of the slate writing board. This was a small slate board that was placed under the séance table. It had a pedal that was used by the medium, and at the end of the pedal was a piece of chalk. Thus, as you can probably see, the medium would use their foot while engaged in the séance, and this would produce words or pictures that came through from spirits. This have a bad reputation though, because the person that invented it, Henry Slade, was also a well-known fraud that was caught many times. While he was a fraud though, the tool itself can be used in legitimate ways.

A spirit cabinet is also worth discussing here because it is actually quite commonly used still to this day, even though most people are unaware of it. In traditional Spiritualism, a spirit cabinet is just that, a cabinet that the medium goes in to contact spirits. Extending the conversation we had earlier, many times it can be made from a certain type of wood that has properties that you want to invite in, or it could be a type of wood that is sacred to you for some other reason. Usually, none of this was the case though, and I have not seen a lot of emphasis on the types of wood used for spirit cabinets. Yes, this has to be a small space, but it has to be big enough for the medium to occupy. Usually a cabinet big enough for a medium to sit in on a chair is sufficient. The spirit cabinet may seem odd or silly, but it is actually quite common, and many people don't connect the dots, so to speak, so let's take a moment to do that.

Have you ever gotten a flash of insight or a message from a spirit or guide when you were driving or riding in a car? Or, have you ever gotten the same when you were taking a shower? The reason for this is that when you are in a small space like both of those, energy is more concentrated. This allows an easier facilitation for spirit contact. Now do you see what I mean? Thousands if not millions of people experience this all of the time, but they do not know that this is an extension of this metaphysical teaching. Fewer, still, know of this tie to Spiritualism, but it was Spiritualism that brought this device to the masses. Friends of mine and I have a running joke about this because it is so common. We like to call the car the "moving (or rolling) spirit cabinet," because so much spirit contact has been made this way over the years.

Many other tools exist, such as tarot cards, but they are by and large from other cultures and traditions, and while Spiritualism may have broadened their exposure to the masses, they already existed beyond the scope of Spiritualism. In other words, while many Spiritualists used the tarot, it was already around long before them, and was found in enough spiritual traditions that it was not that big of a deal, to put it bluntly. This point is worth mentioning because you may discover other spiritual contact tools out there that I don't discuss here, and this may be because I do not know them, or they are more aligned with other spiritual traditions more so than Spiritualism. Yes, you can still use them for your spirit contact sessions, and I encourage you to explore the divinatory tools that align with your spiritual path. Since this is a treatise on spirit guides specifically, I will not stray too far into the realm of divination, although if you feel to expand that direction to improve your spirit guide contact, feel free to do so. There is a lot of value in incorporating such things, and this adds a personal touch to your work, which makes the spirit guide connection deeper.

Techniques

We will shift our focus now to various techniques. The first one to discuss is a spirit portrait. In short, a person opens their clairvoyant senses and draws what they see, as if they were drawing or painting a portrait of the spirit. This is usually done with various mediums, ranging from oil paintings to pastel charcoals and chalks. Oftentimes this is done for someone that wants to see their spirit guides, but today, many people do this regarding non-spirt guide spirits that they encounter. This is another idea and technique that has been around long before Spiritualism, and can be found in various global cultures dating back thousands of years, but with the development of Spiritualism, this technique found a wider audience. I am careful to avoid saying that the person doing the artwork is an artist because I have known several people over the years that had no artistic training and very little artistic skill yet could draw some of the most beautiful spiritual impressions that I have seen. For some, developing this technique led them to develop their artistry skills in general outside of mediumship work like this, but others did not explore its development outside of spirit portraits. Sometimes this is known as automatic drawing, and one of the masters of that skill was the occultist Austin Osman Spare.

A related technique is that of automatic writing. To do

this, you open yourself up to the spirits, and, armed with pencil (or pen) and paper, you allow yourself to write whatever comes through. A good way to do this is to put your mind elsewhere, while your hand, arm, and body, go through the process of writing the information down. So, one way you could do it would be to watch an uplifting movie while absentmindedly writing down what comes through, and then to evaluate it when you are done. I have had great fun with this over the years, but it does take a lot of practice to disassociate your mind while you are doing this. Obsessing over the results will only work against you.

As mentioned in the tools section, I will not wander too far down the rabbit hole of various divination techniques, but there are some worth mentioning, and a lot more can easily be found with minimal research. The first one that comes to mind as an example is cloud gazing, also known as "nephomancy," but there is an extensive list of divinatory practices you can employ as you develop your spirit guide relationships. All of these fall under the broad category of techniques, but not all of them are related to Spiritualism, although even that point could be argued.

Structure

One of the biggest gifts Spiritualism has given to the Western Esoteric Tradition is a system that can be used to work with not only spirit guides, but also spirits in general. This makes it one of the most put-together occult systems in existence today. It is this structure that we will be discussing over the course of the rest of the book, as we go into great depth and detail about the four primary spirit guides that are found in Spiritualism. Besides this psychospiritual structure though, Spiritualism also gives us information to use when it comes to spirit contact in general. These two points are very interesting to me, because they can be grafted onto any spiritual system out there, and in that way, are more in line with spiritual technology rather than matters of faith. Yes, this does mean that Spiritualism does have dogma attached to it, but there is very little dogma, and the dogma that exists is rooted in metaphysics rather than beliefs.

Before Spiritualism, guide and spirit work was highly subjective and contextual to the spiritual tradition of the seeker. This is fine on a personal scale, and even regional scale, but once you get into the global interconnectedness that exists and is growing every day, we can easily see the potential for miscommunications and misunderstandings. This does not mean other traditions are wrong, but rather I mention this here to highlight the necessity of a structure like this to establish a communal spiritual language.

This does require a brief segue though, as there is something important to note for those that want to explore Spiritualism further on their own. When you begin to read other books on Spiritualism, you will see a heavy emphasis on Christianity. This is a by-product of its time and can be easily altered or removed altogether. But when you do that, you also depart from traditional Spiritualism, and move more into Independent Spiritualism. Ideas such as God, Jesus, and other Christian concepts are readily found in Spiritualist writings, but as Dion Fortune discussed in her classic, "Spiritualism and Occultism," a creative mind can easily work around these ideas if they are not of that persuasion.

In Spiritualism, you have four primary spirit guides, and they are located at specific places in proximity to you. Your gatekeeper guide, also known as your guardian guide, is located in front of you. Your master teacher guide is located behind you. Your Doctor of Philosophy guide is located on your right, and your Doctor of Chemistry guide to your left. The placement of all four of these make sense but do still require a brief discussion. You can see why the gatekeeper guide is standing in front of you. It is their job to protect you from things coming your way, so much like Set in the ancient Egyptian stories, it goes out in front as you go through life. The placement of the master teacher guide also stands to reason, in that it is behind you because it is overlighting you and your life.

The other two guides, though, may require some adjustment in your personal practice. Their locations are based on classic metaphysics, which tells us that the right side of the body corresponds to the mental plane and the mind, whereas the left side of the body corresponds to the astral plane and emotions. The point to know here though, is that this system of correspondences is based on someone *being right-handed!* Most of the world is right-handed after all, so this is not that big of a piece of dogma, but if you are left-handed (like I am), then reversing their position not only makes sense, it is in line with who you are. If someone is right-handed, then it is clear that the right side of the body which corresponds to the mental plane, also corresponds to their dominant hand. Thus, by default, the Doctor of Chemistry, corresponding to emotions and the astral plane, aligns with their "off-hand." So, if one is left-handed, reversing the guides is in line with the essence of the spiritual law, and not the letter of it.

To clarify, I am left-handed, and because of this, my Doctor of Philosophy guide is to my left. My Doctor of Chemistry guide is to my right. This is in conflict with a lot of classic Spiritualist material that was written and released over the last one hundred and fifty years, but this does not mean it is wrong. Remember that earlier I demonstrated the interconnectedness between Spiritualism and metaphysics, and this statement that I made honors the metaphysical principles that Spiritualism is built on, but at the same time shows that there is not one specific way to apply those principles. In my personal scheme, the gatekeeper guide and master teacher guide are still located in their respective places.

If you are ambidextrous, then yes, technically, it is your choice where the guides go, but if you have the choice, it would be wise to keep the guides where they are classically located, with the Doctor of Philosophy to your right and the doctor of chemistry to your left. This not only aligns you with Spiritualism in a technical sense, it also keeps you aligned with classic metaphysics, too. In a broad sense, this allows you to tap into greater pools of gnosis and wisdom, because that is the basic nature of the egregore, and us left-handers have to adapt to meet the egregore on the level.

I realize that in this section I may have thrown a lot of terms and titles your way that you may not be familiar with, but over the course of the rest of the book, we will go into great detail discussing them, so please don't let this point bother you too much. I am dedicating a chapter to each guide, as well as other spirit guides, so all will be made clear (If I do my job right!) by the end of the book.

Frequently Asked Questions

Finally, let's close this chapter by addressing some frequently asked questions I have gotten over the last fifteen years or so.

A. *Does this discussion mean that spirit guides have just now come into being*? The answer to that is a resounding no. Spirit guides have been around for a long, long time. The gift that Spiritualism gave metaphysics is a way to classify and work with these spirits in a structured format.

B. Do my spirit guides have to be human? A: Technically, no, but it is wise to remember the karmic law of attraction, so if we're human, then it stands to reason that they are, too, especially if soul contracts were made before we came down into physical form, which we will discuss in the next chapter. There are a few caveats to this, so let me take a moment to explain. Often times, our primary spirit guides make themselves known to us in ways that we are comfortable with in order to further develop the relationship between us and them. Therefore, they may sometimes appear as deities from our favorite pantheon, or deities that we connect very strongly with so that we feel comfortable working with them. Hence you may have spirit guides early on that look like deities.

C. *Will my spirit guides stay the same in appearance and relationship to me as I grow and evolve?* No, most times they will not. Spirit guides may change their appearance to us as we grow and develop. The four primary guides are with us for the duration of our lives, but may change how they present themselves to us in accord with how open and spiritually evolved we are at any given moment in our lives. It is common for a spirit guide to show us the image of a particular deity until we get to a mental space at which we can see them as "Guide John Public," as an example.

D. *Are there only four guides that each of us have?* No, not at all, and later, we will look at the more specialized guides that one can have while moving through life and fulfilling different roles that may be requested of us at various points.

E. *Do we only have one spirit guide?* This is a misconception that was popularized in the early part of this century. No, we do not only have one spirit guide, but yes, the strong possibility exists that some people will only make contact with one spirit guide, and that is okay.

Chapter Two: Metaphysical Basics

In this chapter we are going to look at what you should consider and do before starting to work with your guides. A lot of the material here will have to do with sacred space creation, for example. If you have read "Spirit Relations," then you already know a lot of this material. Besides sacred space creation, we will discuss *why* and *how* spirit guides are connected to us. While I am doing my best to keep things dogma-lite or even dogma-free, there will also be times when I feel this cannot be done, and this is one such time. The first point we will address is our connection with our guides, and the piece of dogma that goes with this is that they are connected to us karmically, which means in my mind, you have to believe in karma in order to work with this material.

Yes, there are guides that you can work with that are not karmically connected to you, but after working with them, a karmic connection will be established both ways. These karmic relationships are established on the other side of the veil before your soul comes down into physical form for this incarnation. The relationship between your incarnated personality self and your spirit guides is one that was decided upon before birth, when the soul's path was being charted this time around. By extension, though, you can also see that you have to believe in the spirit world in order to work with spirit guides and this material. I assume both of the above points are true if you have made it this far in the book, but I also feel that this needs mentioning just to keep things transparent.

***

Karmic Connections

A common first thought about spirit guides is "why?" Why do we have them? How are we connected to them, and them, us? Why work with them? These and many other questions come up when we are first starting out with them, and a lot of the answers can be easily explained. To think that spirit guides are connected with us only during this lifetime is only partially true, as we will discuss here, and this is also the reason why one has to believe in the spiritual world in order to truly work with them.

Relationships with your spirit guides are established before birth, when both the guides and the soul of yourself are in spirit. Really, there are two ways to view this. This relationship may either be karmic in nature, or an agreed upon arrangement that is new to this lifetime. Coming into this lifetime there may be some relationship, karmic in nature, that is held over from a previous lifetime, and it is decided that harmonizing the situation will occur in this lifetime through the role of the spirit guide. Or it could be that the spirit was familial in another life, and now the greatest learning and growth can be achieved through this association while you are in physical form. For example, perhaps you had a child in a previous lifetime, and that relationship was unbalanced for various reasons. Then, in this lifetime, the dynamic between guide and incarnated soul is decided upon because it is the most effective way for both to grow. Or, it could be that in another life, you and your spirit guide were lovers, and this path forward seems the best for healing as well as growth. You can now see that there is no limit to the nature of the relationships, and it can also be seen that this is highly subjective material. That is why I use examples to illustrate points, rather than giving you strict, inflexible dogma. The fact of the matter is, no one really knows, but what I offer here are plausible explanations and situations to consider.

Ultimately, only by discussing it with your spirit guides can you find out your personal truth (and theirs!).

However, conversely, the relationship between guide and manifested human could also be a brand-new relationship that is beginning with this incarnation. I will use another example here to illustrate the point. Let's say that while your soul was in spirit, it realized that it had spent many lifetimes in a monastic setting. Because of this, continual vows of poverty were taken. Once the soul realizes this, it may try and seek out another soul that is good with money, to act as a spirit guide for them in this lifetime. But that spirit has its own agenda, and should get something out of the relationship, too. So, the two spirits decide the nature of their relationship for this lifetime. The spirit that will be incarnated will have the other spirit as a spirit guide, and specifically as a Doctor of Philosophy guide. Why this particular station, you ask? If a person is good with money, then they understand principles of manifestation, prosperity, logic, and reason. They are also probably pretty insightful when it comes to dealing with other people, and all of these are traits of the mental plane. In exchange for this spirit taking on the role of the Doctor of Philosophy, the incarnated soul will introduce it to spiritual themes, concepts, and lifestyles, so that when the guide soul comes down into physical form, they will get more personal growth, and on a deeper level. I realize this is a very simplistic example, but I hope it illustrates the point. This is but one example of a new relationship between an incarnated soul and a spirit guide, rather than a relationship held over from a previous life.

This idea is one that has been a popular subject over the last twenty years or so, and these are spirit contracts. The premise for them is simple: When spirits are in spirit form, before birth, spirit contracts are made between various spirits for various reasons. Most of this recent discussion has been based on spirit guides and on explaining why some things in the world are the way they are, but to the seasoned occultist, this idea has been around for centuries longer in the form of pact magick. Bluntly put, pact magick is when a magician creates a pact with a spirit in order to achieve a particular goal. This idea has been blown out of proportion through various forms of entertainment and religion over the years in the form of one selling their soul to the devil in exchange for power, so the idea of spirit contracts is not new, but the new information on them is more enlightened, and covers more than just the stereotype I share above. This repackaging has introduced the material to the greater masses in an easily digestible way, and in general, that is a good thing. Many people think pacts are always negative, but they don't have to be. Many of them can be quite beneficial when worked with properly and in a healthy manner.

Basically, these relationships come down to negotiation, mediation, and balancing things out from previous lives, or initiating new ways in this one. It is worth clarifying this point because there are some people out there that believe our spirit guides are given to us, or ordained to us, by some external deity or some other such spirit. If that idea is part of your belief system and it works for you in your overall spiritual growth and greatest good, then okay, that works for you, and there is nothing wrong with that. But, for those of you that are reading this that don't believe in that concept, please don't force yourself to adopt that concept for your spiritual growth and development with your spirit guides. Truth is, this whole, brief tangent is subjective and personal, and I simply put this paragraph in here to clear the air about things you may read other places.

By extension, this also means that physical relationships we have in this lifetime may turn into spirit guide relationships in another life. The souls involved may even take turns through the course of many lives, alternating back and forth between incarnations, sharing the role of guide to one another. I have met and spoken with many people that have said this is the nature of their relationships with their spirit guides, and usually this has a familiar trait to it. In one life, one soul is the parent and the other the child, and in this life, one or the other stays in spirit to guide the other. Again, as you can see, a lot of this is subjective and open to interpretation, but they are points to consider nonetheless.

Exercise One: Let's address our first exercise of the book. If you have spirit guides, what is the nature of your relationship with them, as defined by the material in this chapter up to this point? If you do not speculate on this, then feel free to meditate on it to gain further insight. If you do not currently work with spirit guides, then simply keep this information in mind as you begin to grow and unfold. Make sure to record these initial thoughts in your journal for future reference.

Preparation for Spirit Guide Work

When you decide to seriously begin working with your spirit guides, it is wise to practice sacred space creation. Over time and with experience, you can alter this, and in some cases even cease to use it, but when you are first starting out, this is what I consider a necessary skill to develop. There are multiple reasons to do this. First, let's look at the psychological factor. Whenever you create sacred space, you are telling your mind that you are about to do something sacred, something different. Therefore, the more you create sacred space, the more you build the idea in your mind that when you are doing it, a different part of your mind is triggered to life. Parts of your mind, and thus you, are going to be developed that are not part of your daily consciousness.

Secondly, from an energetic perspective, you are cleansing an area and preparing to invite spirits in so that you can achieve results that are of a more spiritual nature. Keep in mind here that when we are saying spiritual nature, we mean ideas and beings that are of the spirit side of life. That is all. You are removing unwanted, accumulated negative energetics from a physical space to make the space more inviting to certain kinds of spirits, in this case your spirit guides. Many books have been written about the subject, and I discuss it in other books, such as "Spirit Relations," so there is plenty of material present, but I do want to give you these thoughts so that you can get started right away.

Before we get to that, though, we should start by focusing on the self and everything related to you. Make sure that you are of a clear mind, to begin. Doing spirit guide work when under emotional duress is unwise, as it is unwise to do it when under emotional extremes of any nature. It is also wise to avoid being too full in the stomach. The traditional teaching here is to avoid eating, particularly meat, immediately before you do spirit work, because this serves to anchor your mind into your body, and you want it closer to out of the body for your work. Next, make sure that your mind is clear. Distractions caused by work and other everyday concerns should not interfere with your spirit work. Yes, we will all have those days and challenges associated with this, so I know it is an ongoing process, but keeping it in mind when you are initially starting can save a lot of self-doubt. When all of these are addressed, it is time to create the space and set the stage.

You will need a small room to execute this work. This does not have to be a room dedicated solely to spirit work, but it does help if you have this resource. The more you use a particular space for spirit contact, the more the energies build up there, and the more comfortable the spirits become, so that it is easier to make contact and exchanges in general. If you do not have a room to dedicate to this work, you can simply pick a room that has a door that can be locked. Privacy is of paramount importance, and let's face facts. If your life is not together enough that you can manifest being in a locked room by yourself for a few minutes a day to work on spirit contact, then there are far more severe and worse problems in your life, and spirit guide work should probably be set aside until you address these subjects. In this room, a chair, table, your journal, a pen, and either an oil lamp or candles should be present. The chair and table should be there for obvious reasons, but let's talk about candles and oil lamps.

While candles and/or oil lamps are the traditional and suggested lighting sources for this work, you should know why this is, so that if you cannot use candles or lamps for whatever reasons, you can adjust according to their metaphysical functions. Yes, a good, flickering candle flame is always nice for these situations, but you can achieve the same effect by knowing that it is simply the brightness and starkness of the light that should be taken into account. If you use a room where the lighting is the same as it is in your mundane life, it will be harder to achieve spirit contact. One reason for this is that there is no mental shift into a liminal state. Another reason for this is that the majority of lights today are fluorescent or halogen, two materials that are not good for spirit work. Both oil and wax have lower melting points than the other two, which means they are better vessels for messages from spirit. They are also more organic, so they have a stronger connection to the spirit realm. If you cannot have candles or an oil lamp for various reasons, then find another substitute that is not fluorescent or halogenic, and that substitute also has to be of a liminal nature. Low-light situations are good for creating this effect, and yes, sometimes I have use fluorescent lighting that was on a dimmer switch. I simply dimmed the lights to a level that I thought was appropriate. It was low-light, and even though it was fluorescent, this was offset by the liminal nature of the lighting.

Sacred Space Creation

Often times the concept of creating sacred space is discussed, but is never really detailed. At first it seems nebulous, but once we take a closer look, we see that it can be quite easy to achieve. There are many different facets to it, and this brings us here. When you first start doing guide work, sacred space is essential in my opinion. This is especially true if one has no experience in this life area. Once you develop your relationship with your guides, the creation of sacred space takes a back seat to the relationship itself. We will look at this material from the perspective of the planes to make it easier to digest and reference.

The Physical Plane

There are a lot of different perspectives on the physical tools that it takes to create sacred space on the physical plane, and a lot of these have to do with the spiritual beliefs of an individual. What works for the Buddhist is not the same as what works for the Pagan. However, there are a few underlying factors to be aware of when you are creating sacred space.

A common denominator is the purification of a physical space so that one can work closer with the spirit world. There are two major reasons for this. The first reason is that by creating sacred space, you are shifting your consciousness. The shift of consciousness that is occurring has to do with training your mind to enter into an altered state of consciousness separated away from daily activities. When sacred space is created, the mind is understanding that now it is entering into a different relationship with a different part of the multiverse. The second reason is to cleanse an area of undesirable influences that are not conducive to spiritually themed work. This is where the true art comes into play because this idea relies heavily upon one's spiritual paradigm. What may be an undesirable influence to some may not be an undesirable influence to another. This is also where we get into tools and how to use them, which will be the next point discussed. A detail point here to be aware of is that there are two very different schools of thought that have to do with physical sacred space that should be considered. The first school of thought is that you dedicate a physical space in your home for spiritually themed work, and you use that exclusively to the best of your abilities. What this does is build up the connection with spirit, thereby creating a chamber to work in that has strength in proportion to the amount of spiritual work done there. Hence you are creating a vessel through which it becomes very easy to work with spirit due to the fact that the energy used adds up over time. The alternating school of thought is that after you do your spiritual work, you banish or cleanse the space back to the way it was before you did the working, thus removing influences that were just worked with. Hence if you use a room that isn't dedicated to spiritual work, you simply reset the energy to the way it was before you began the work. These two approaches can be used together, though, and that is important to note that they aren't mutually exclusive. Often times one will have a physical space dedicated to spiritual work yet use banishings and other cleansings to reset the energy of the chamber after each interaction with spirit. This is especially important to know if one works with grey magick. For example, you don't necessarily want lingering influences of a dark creature or nature hanging around when you work with higher vibrational light beings, but it is wise to use the same chamber for both to add to its spiritual strength and what it has to offer, as listed above. Now that we've discussed theory, let's look at practice.

The use of physical plane tools assists in the shift of consciousness as well as grounding the energy down and bringing things into manifestation. Using tools can be as elaborate or as simple as you want them to be. The first point to consider is incense. There are many different kinds of incense that can be particularly useful to create sacred space. Another point to mention here is that there is usually a debate as to whether or not to use the actual pure extract, or if a synthetic scent is just as valid. While the pure extract is always preferred, it is just as valid to work with synthetics. The reason for this is that it is the scent that triggers the mind, so it can be equally effective. There are also probably other forms of incenses from other cultures, but I am unaware of them, so feel free to do your research. It has also been scientifically proven that scent is the strongest sense associated with memory, which helps build up the energy in your chamber due to the consciousness shift mentioned above. By extension then, you can also use oils, either essential or synthetic, as a substitute for incense. Generally, the scents of incense and oils are the same, so if you have a favorite incense, you can usually find the oil equivalent. Let's look at some of the more common and popular scents to use.

Sage and smudging are the first things we will address. This comes to us from several native American traditions. Using either California white sage or desert sage to cleanse a space of negativity are two common methods to use, but you can also use Mugwort or other sacred herbs of your choosing, as long as their properties have to do with cleansing and preparing a space for ritual work. More accurately, sage, or the smudging process, cleanses a room of negativity. However, since it is a Native American tradition, it would be wise to use it predominantly on the North American continent. Most cultures have their own version of sage. For example, in Central and South America, Copal is used in the same fashion. What's interesting about sage though, is that recent studies have said that it does kill harmful airborne bacteria, so it is also healthy.

The next one we will address is Dragon's Blood. Dragon's Blood incense is a derivative of the sap from the Dragon's Blood tree that comes from Southeast Asia and Africa. A word of caution is important here though, because if you touch Dragon's Blood itself, it can be toxic in large doses, so it is wise to wash your hands after each use. Dragon's Blood purifies and exorcises, and thus it is perfect for removing unwanted energetics.

Following that up, we will turn our attention to a long-standing classic blend, that of Frankincense & Myrrh. This is a cleansing blend that comes from ancient Egypt but has been made famous by the Catholic Church over the centuries. Usually the two are used together, but sometimes it is wise to use one or the other. Frankincense removes negativity and helps to raise the vibration of the area to a higher level. Myrrh helps to ground, and in this way invites spirit into the area for more concrete manifestations. A tangent here is that both are routinely used to contact solar deities specifically, which is a teaching that comes from ancient Egypt.

Another alternative to consider is using misters. Many oils can be diluted in water and then sprayed about. This has become quite popular over the last several years, and they are relatively easy to make by yourself. On one level, using a mister rather than incense is activating a higher vibration, since the incense is more earthy, but for what we are discussing here, it really doesn't matter. I have made several misters in the past, both for creating sacred space and for specific ritual purposes. There are many different ways to make them, and simple research can reveal them, but I will share the formula I use here. The ration is to fill a mister bottle with two-thirds water, the remaining third witch hazel, and then add in the oil that you want. There is no amount of oil to be used, but I would suggest using a small amount, rather than going heavy with it. This is because oil is thicker than water and can congeal. This is also the function of the witch hazel, to make sure the oil is diffused through all of the water rather than globbing together. So, the more oil you use, the more likely it is that it will pool up. Because this is not an exact science, you may find you spend a decent amount of time experimenting, and that is okay. Each time, before you use it, make sure to shake the bottle to make sure the diffusion is as good as you can make it.

You can probably see then that an oil diffuser can be just as effective. I have used oil diffusers many times and have had much success with them. This is a good middle-of-the-road solution if you want oils and a similar effect to misters, but you can't buy one or make your own. It doesn't matter whether you use a diffuser that uses electricity or candles, so go with the choice that makes the most sense and is best for you.

Himalayan salt requires a bit of a conversation here, too. Himalayan salt and salt lamps have gained popularity over the last several years for a variety of reasons. Himalayan salt generates negative ions, which help enhance the spiritual experience and contact. Often it is good to have it sitting in your sacred space, even if it is just a piece of the salt itself. Yes, it is always good to have it turned on if it is a lamp or a candle holder, but it is not necessary. It is not a "cure all" or ultimate tool like some people may think, but it can be very useful when used as we are discussing.

***

The Emotional Plane

Now we will shift our focus to the inner life and inner planes in preparation for spirit guide contact. While the physical side of sacred space is important, without addressing our inner life we would be using an empty shell. A large part of the success of a working is dependent on the emotional involvement you have. If you go through the motions but never get fully emotionally invested in it, then there is no fuel to propel you forward. The first point to address is emotionally centering yourself. Sometimes your sacred space is the place where you can emotionally release whatever it is that's troubling you. This is all well and good, but if you do this, remember to cleanse and smudge afterwards so that the residual emotional energy doesn't negatively influence future workings in an unintended way. If you are emotionally out of sorts, it is wise to get a handle on that before attempting any kind of spirit contact, as mentioned above. You may want to engage in physical activity to burn the energy out before working with spirit. One of the ways to do this is to feel the adrenaline that rises, and to recognize the sensations in your body in an effort to separate the emotions from the physical sensation. By identifying them, you then gain power over them. Sometimes it's better to sleep on it rather than emotionally react to a situation as well. Before working with your guides, address all of these points, just to be safe.

It is also wise to remember that emotions are food, and that there are beings out there that feed off of that. Thus, by controlling our emotions we protect our energetic selves. The more you work with your spirit guides, the more this idea and how it is handled will change, so just know that this is a situation that can be managed and handled.

Water is excellent for detoxifying the body, and while it

is good to drink often, it is especially good to drink before ritual. Just make sure to drink it far enough in advance that you don't have to go to the bathroom during your working. The human body is mostly made of water, and water acts as a conduit between the planes, so being properly hydrated can open yourself up to the finer energies you will be contacting.

Let's turn our attention to music now. Even though we hear music, and thus it can be considered part of the physical plane, really, music triggers emotions. An uplifting song can brighten your day, but also if you are emotionally out of sorts, you can listen to music that identifies with you, or that allows you to vent that energy. Choosing the right music is very important, and as a general rule of thumb it is wise to choose music that doesn't have lyrics in it because they can be very distracting, or not in line with what you're doing. Music with lyrics can be useful though if each and every lyric is in line with your intent. If you can find traditional music of a nature that is in line with your intent, then even better. For example, when working with spirit guides, oftentimes Spiritualism classics such as "Revive Us Again" are appropriate. However, sometimes silence is just as effective as music, so consider whether or not to use music before choosing the music you want to use.

The Mental Plane

This is the plane that is the most important above all else when it comes to sacred space creation because in a pinch, this is all you need to create it. The mind should be clear of emotional influences not connected with the working, unless the work requires them. The mental plane is the plane of logic, reason, discipline, and self-confidence, among other characteristics. Abstract thinking is also a trait of this plane, as is mathematics. We will now discuss some common mental plane traits, and specifically how they come into play when creating sacred space for spirit guide work.

First, let us discuss discipline. The mind should be disciplined to alleviate all intrusions of thoughts that are not connected with the working. By seeing your thoughts from an outside perspective, you can gain greater control over your inner self-talk, which is a differentiating factor for success. In short, if you doubt your ability to manifest, then it won't. If you second guess your work, you will most likely end up with diluted results. If your mind is constantly wandering during the working, don't be surprised if the results are not clear cut and delineated. I discuss self-talk, as well as the power of words in general, in my book "Vocal Magick," the first one of this series, if you want to know more about this.

The next point to consider is that of rising above emotions. Part of this was discussed previously, but another factor is to remember to do the emotions and not let them do you. If you experience something in your sacred space, remember that it is there through the karmic law of attraction, and thus it got a foot hold into your space through something in your auric field. This does not mean have no emotions, but rather, to make sure your emotional control is as sharp as it can be so as not to affect your results.

Keep your mind focused on all facets of the working, whether this is the symbolism present, or symbolism that is not visibly present yet related to the situation. The essence of this is concentration. Being able to concentrate is a tantamount skill for success when you are working with your guides, at least at first. This means that before you begin your guide work, you may have to develop the skill of concentration, and if this is the case, I encourage you to do so before continuing.

When possible, extend your senses as far as you can

around your personal space to sense for other energetic beings. Also pay attention to the more analytical side of things, like temperature changes and visual anomalies. This concept holds true for your other five senses, and their "clair" counterparts, as discussed in "Spirit Relations." By paying attention to your environment, you are using critical thinking, because you are able to differentiate between an actual spirit message, and a noise outside from a neighbor that is doing housework. I know too many stories of people thinking they had powerful manifestations from spirit, when in reality it was something mundane. A good example of this is if you notice that the temperature drops in the room, be sure to check the thermostat to make sure that wasn't the cause.

Let's take a quick tangent on the topic of temperature changes in the room. Many times, and in many different sources, it is touted that if there is a chill in the room, that is a sign of a spirit being present, or something related to spirits. From decades of experience, I can tell you this is not true. Yes, if you do notice a shift in the air while doing your work, that is an indicator of shifting energy. But, if a spirit is really present and affecting your environment, then the next thing to note is whether the temperature is going up or going down. If it is getting colder in the room, this means that you and others present (if any) are projecting their energy out to the degree that it is lowering the temperature of your body. True spirit presence will raise the temperature in the room because their presence elevates the temperature in much the same way as adding another person into a crowded room makes things hotter (and many times, more uncomfortable!). This is a profound metaphysical teaching, because it serves to remind us that the only difference between us and spirits is that we have physical form and they do not. Otherwise, most of the time, they are just like us, which is particular true when it comes to spirit guides. Yes, they have certain senses that we do not have because they are not confined to the physicality of it all, but their psychology is the same as ours. This is true when working with spirit guides, but if you work with spirits that are more or different, such as gods, goddesses, and other similar beings, then you may find this is not the case.

Finally, if possible, stimulate your third eye ahead of time. The third eye is a vertical eye in a small slit, located in the middle of your forehead, in between both eyes, directly above the top of your nose bridge. Generally it is associated with Hinduism, but the idea can be found in various spiritual traditions and cultures. It is the seat of clairvoyance and corresponds to the pineal gland. A quick side note here is that the endocrine system is one of significance when it comes to spiritual work, but that could take a whole book to discuss. I simply reference it here for those of you that would like to explore it not only as a way to stimulate your third eye, but also to improve the quality of your life in general. There is more to your third eye than just developing it, like most people think. After it is developed, it should be exercised regularly to maintain the work you have done with it. Entire books have been written about it, and I discuss it in greater detail as it pertains to the chakra system in "Spirit Relations."

The Spiritual Plane

The spiritual plane is usually the easiest to work with, and is comprised of our spiritual tapestry. Because of this, it is largely subjective to the individual, which means there is not a lot I can say about it. It would be pointless and fruitless to cover every spiritual system that is out there. However, there are a few details to know to flesh out your spirit guide experience. These are details to consider. One thing is true above all else: have a belief system, even if that system is you at the top of the pyramid.

Many spiritual traditions have guardian spirits that you can call on, and if you feel it appropriate, call them in before you start your work. For example, in Christianity, you could call on Archangel Michael, or all of the four major archangels in the Western Esoteric Tradition. When first developing spirit guide contact, you may want to invite them in until you find your rhythm. Yes, this can also be part of your working, but I mention it here as a separate event because it may make you more comfortable, at least initially. If you do not work with guardians in this fashion, you can still call in other guardians, such as the virtues of courage, willpower, and ability. These should be ones that you work with on a regular basis and that you have an established rapport.

In short, the essence of spiritual plane preparation is to make sure you are spiritually sound, grounded, and focused. How you do that is subjective, but it does require addressing before you begin guide contact. If you are an atheist, you can use the idea above about calling on virtues and character traits. Regardless of how you do this, it would be wise to do it none the less.

Spirit Guide Contact, a Template

I realize that I threw a lot of stuff at you in this chapter, and some of it may not make sense if it is outside your spiritual paradigm, so let's detail everything out. This is a template you can use when you are first developing guide contact, and I do hope that over time you can adapt this to your specific situation and spiritual paradigm. If you choose not to though, feel free to continue to use this one. I have been using this as a base template for decades, and have had success with it. It is my wish that you have success with it, too!

Step One: Timing: I have not discussed this in this book yet, but the comments on it are brief, so we will cover them now. Knowing when to act is important as knowing how to act, and when you are first starting spirit guide work, it is wise to align your working with the phases of the moon. The impact and power of the moon has been known about for centuries and can be used to achieve more success than you thought possible. As you begin your spirit guide work, it is wise to align with the full moon. This is when more power is in the air than normal. This is also when one is more in-tune with their psychic skills, and those same skills are also amplified. If you cannot do the work on the exact day of the full moon, that is okay. The day before the full moon, the day of the full moon, and the day after the full moon, are all acceptable times. If this is still not possible, then you can do your work sometime between the new moon and the full moon. This period of time is known as the waxing moon, and this means that the energy in the air is building from weak to strong.

Step Two: Location: Remember what was discussed above about the physical space you are going to use, and before the work, prepare it as previously discussed. Make sure to have a chair, table, light source, aroma source, pen or pencil, paper, and some sort of communication device, whether it is a spirit board, crystal ball, black mirror, or some other medium that we covered earlier in this chapter. The only tool to avoid using is a pendulum. The reason for this is that a pendulum taps into the subconscious predominantly, rather than focusing on external spirits like we are addressing here. Also remember to turn off your phone (Not set to silent, actually turn it off), adjust your lighting, and ignite the smells. If you are using music, also start it now.

Step Three (Optional): Call in your Guardians: If you would like to call in guardians to assist with this work, now would be the time to do that. The easiest way to do this is through one of the five modes of prayer that are commonly used. Another way to do this is through invocation, where you invite the guardian "into" you, meaning that they share your consciousness to protect and guide you. Below is a sample prayer. It is always better if you write your own, but this can be used as a starting point. You can also feel free to use prayers from other sources if they would be more appropriate.

[Insert name of guardian/guardians here], I call to you tonight to bless and protect this work. May your presence serve to elevate the energy in the room, and to drive away the unbalanced and negative. With your protection and guidance, I further my spiritual development as a healthy, whole, being. [Insert name of guardian/guardians here], bless, consecrate, and protect this rite as I move forward with my spiritual evolution. In your name and in the name of all that is holy, I thank you for your attendance and assistance.

A slight tangent should be discussed here, just for clarification. Some people work with a patron deity, and if this is your case, you can call on them rather than particular guardians. Simply insert their name in the above prayer where applicable.

If you would rather invoke the guardian (or deity) into you, then you can use the following invocation, if you do not have a preferred one.

[Insert name here] I invoke you tonight for your guidance, wisdom, and power. May you help me as I further my own spiritual development. As you help me, may you receive blessings of the most high. [Insert name here], I welcome you into my mind and body, so that together, we contact those guides around me that can assist my spiritual growth and greatest good.

Traditional invocations may also include titles and traits of the spirit you are invoking, and if this is your case, feel free to insert them in the above template where appropriate and applicable.

Step Four: Creating Sacred Space: We discussed the pieces of this earlier, and now it is time to put those into practice. Usually, this begins in the east, but you can begin at other directions if they are in line with your spiritual beliefs. In the Western Esoteric Tradition, a lot of emphasis is put on aligning ourselves with the physical world by aligning ourselves with the four cardinal directions of the compass. Each direction corresponds to a particular element, and therefore a particular plane of the ones we previously discussed. The east corresponds to the element of air and the plane of the mind. The south corresponds to the element of fire and the spiritual plane. The west corresponds to the element of water, and the emotional plane, and the north corresponds to the element of earth and the physical plane. There is a caveat here though, which is that these are the correspondences for those that live north of the equator. South of the equator is a different story.

This is a point that I can only partially address though, as I do not live south of the equator. Friends of mine that do have often given me these correspondences, but I do not know of any one set that is accepted by everyone, so you may want to do your research on this, or just use the correspondences I shared above. I just feel this is important enough to mention here for the sake of completeness.

If you struggle with which direction is where, you can use a compass to find this out, or if you don't have access to that, you can create what is known as "magical directions." This means that you simply declare a direction in your room as east, regardless of whether it really is or not. Then, at a ninety degree angle, the next direction would be south. Then, ninety degrees from there would be west, and ninety degrees from there would be north. From north, ninety degrees would bring you back to east, completing your circle.

Now that we have that established, let's move on to the actual procedure. In your hand, have the stick of incense, or incense censer if you are using incense that burns on charcoal. Or, if you are using oils, have that receptacle in hand. In some spiritual practices, the censer or stick of incense is used to trace a particular holy symbol of that faith in the air while speaking. I leave that out here, but if you feel so inclined to do so, then feel free. You would begin tracing it when you start speaking the words. Face east, and confidently state: *"In the name of the spirits of the east and the element of air, I consecrate this space as clear and unblemished."* Turn to your right so that you are facing south, then confidently state: *"In the name of the spirits of the south and the element of fire, I consecrate this space from this earth to the highest planes above."* Turn to your right so that you are facing west and confidently state: *"In the name of the spirits of the west and the element of water, I consecrate this space. May it be cleansed of all impurities, and may my work be carried to the finer planes."* Turn to your right so that you are facing north and confidently state: *"In the name of the spirits of the north and the element of earth, I consecrate this space. May my work here be made manifest in my daily life so that it brings abundance in mind, body, and spirit."* Finally, turn so that you are facing east again, but now, turn so that you are facing your table and chair setup, and confidently state: *"In the name of the holiest spirits and most pure beings, I invite you into this chamber. May our work together bring uplifting results so that I can evolve on my spiritual path for the greatest growth and good of all beings, both physical and not."* When all of this is done, put the aroma maker on the table, but out of the way.

As you can see, if you use incense, the room might get excessively smoky, so you may want to give this piece of the template a trial run or two before doing it live. One of the most depressing things that can happen is that the incense smoke from this interferes with your spirit work. That can be very frustrating. But then again, having some smoke in the air add to the mystique of it all, and can even help bring messages through from the finer planes. Also keep all of this in mind if you have breathing problems, or are living with someone that does, because all of this may cause problems, which would go against the nature of this work.

There are many, many, MANY variations on this basic consecration, so feel free to research and adapt it to your personal preference. What I offer here is a common, basic structure, but I have seen countless adaptations of this, so once you find your rhythm, it would be wise to tailor make this to your spiritual paradigm. Remember the mental plane concept of discipline too. The more you continually use a particular cleansing practice, the more power is generated, and the more the whole chamber is made strong and defined. Yes, changing this from time to time is good, but only if your changes reflect the changes in your spiritual path, and are not done just because.

Step Five: The Work: Now we come to the actual spirit guide contact. A lot of this will be determined by the tool that you use for contact, so as much as I would like to go into detail, it is too hard and cumbersome to do for the sake of this book. Instead, I will focus on principles that transcend the medium used. Now that you have established sacred space, it is time to engage the guide. Once you are seated, meditate, using the music or the silence to center your mind. You may begin receiving messages that way, and if you do, then record your answers in your journal. If you do not receive messages that way, then pick up your chosen tool and use it. Here is the technique I used with a spirit one time. I drew the major arcana cards out of my tarot deck and used the Hebrew letter correspondences to establish a communication channel. You could use that method, or you could use the spirit board, or whatever tool previously discussed. This is why I cannot go into great detail about this, because there is no way I could cover all of the various forms in existence. But this is the step where you would insert this work.

This does not leave the conversation over, though. When you are communicating with this guide, there are several things to address. First, find out its name. It will give you a name to call it. Know ahead of time though, that this may or may not be its real name. That is no cause for concern though, because it is giving you a name to know it by that *you* can identify with, to help you feel comfortable when communicating with it. As I mentioned in the frequently asked questions section of chapter one, a guide may change its appearance and even name that is uses when it connects with you through the course of your life. This is quite common, and the reason this is done is because you are growing and developing as a spirit too. I know many people that are in the early years of their spirit guide work, and their guides are such gods as Isis from ancient Egypt, or Thor from the Norse tradition, or some other popular and common deity. Could this guide be an avatar of the god or goddess in question? Sure, of course! It would be naïve of me to think I would know yes or no regarding that question. But the guide could just as easily be a run-of-the-mill spirit that is using that imagery and symbolism because it wants to connect with you on a personal level and inspire you to continue your work at the same time.

A key point to remember here, is that there is already a connection established with our guides. That connection happened before you were incarnated. This means that this type of spirit work is different from other types. This kind of spirit work is internal in nature, where you are making contact with beings that you are already connected with through karma, and the focus of all of this is for your own growth and development.

When you have its name, ask it for a symbol that will be used whenever it wants to communicate with you. This will be a secret symbol, because it should only be known to the two of you. This can be an image, or a numerical pattern, or a phrase, or something similar, but it has to be unique to just the two of you. And, it should be something that you would not normally come across on a daily basis. For example, if you are into numerology and want to set up a symbol with your guide, you may choose a string of numbers. That in and of itself is fine, but make sure it is not a sequence of numbers that you would normally, regularly, come across. So, you could use your birthday (month and day read as one), but you would probably want to avoid using the number 11, or even 11:11, because these are numbers that you probably encounter on a regular basis. This identifying symbol is not just one that works as a passcode between the two of you, it is also a way that your guide can communicate with you while you are living your daily life. For example, if you are running errands and you see the symbol of that particular guide, then you know that guide is actively around you. If you arrive home later, and it is not clear why you got that message, then it is time to go through this procedure to contact it and see what message it has for you. Nothing happens in a vacuum, so if you get that symbol in daily life, there is a reason for it.

The next topic to address is to learn its role as guide in your life. Ask it what role it fulfills. We will be discussing the stations and roles through the remainder of the text, so it is completely understandable if you want to read that material before doing your first spirit contact session. Usually, if this is your first time doing this kind of spirit work, the Master Teacher guide is the one that will arrive, but this may be altered by your circumstances. For example, if you live in a dangerous neighborhood or have a dangerous profession, your Gatekeeper guide may be the one that arrives first, so keep an open mind when you are listening to the spirit's response.

At this point, let's recap this step. By now, you should have the spirit's name, identifying symbol, and station in your schema of guides. Make sure all of that is recorded in your journal. The next question to ask, if you don't have the answer already, is the appearance of your guide. What do they look like? You can either answer this yourself, or ask them to tell you, depending on the tool for communication you use. Their appearance may be a separate question at this point, or it may already be answered, but regardless, take note of it in your journal. When all of these points are completed, your checklist is complete, so congratulations on your first successful spirit guide contact!

Step Six: Releasing the Sacred Space: When the conversation has ended, it is time to release the energy collected there, and any spirits that might be present. You are not releasing your spirit guide though, so keep that in mind. Rather, as you will see, you are releasing the spirits you invited in, in the first place. Begin by facing the east. It is not necessary to have the incense or oil censer with you, but you can use it if you want. If you traced a holy symbol at the beginning of the ritual, you will trace it here, too, as you confidently state the following: *"I give thanks to you, spirits of the east, for empowering and witnessing this ritual. Stay if you will, go if you will. Thank you, thank you, thank you."* Turn to your right so that you are facing south. If applicable, trace the holy symbol and speak, but if not, then simply confidently state the same phrase you used when addressing the spirits of the east, but just adjust it for the south. When completed, turn to the west, state the same, adjusted phrase. Then, turn to the right and state the same, adjusted phrase. Finally, turn back to the east, but turn your attention to your desk and chair, and confidently state: *"I give thanks to you, holiest of spirits and purest beings. Thank you for empowering, witnessing, and protecting this rite. Thank you, thank you, thank you. Stay if you will, or go if you will."*

Snuff out the incense or oil diffuser, reset the room to normal, and do something to put your attention elsewhere. The worst thing you could do is to sit around and dwell on the work you just did. It is better to put your attention on something as far removed from this as possible. Yes, this template is simplistic, but I hope it serves as a launch pad rather than a cell. Adjust it as you see fit, which also means you will adjust it as you spiritually grow, evolve, and change. Remember that since this working was specifically timed, you can go ahead and plan your next "spiritual date night" now.

This brings us to the end of the preliminary information, so we will now turn our attention to specific types of guides and other spirit associates for the remainder of the book. You can use this template for contacting and working with any of them. There are a few exceptions to this that we will discuss in subsequent chapters, but for the most part, you have everything you need for initial spirit guide work. Those of you that have and have read "Spirit Relations" will find a lot of parallels here and can also see how this work coincides with that book, so feel free to combine the material in these two books for a fully developed spiritual contact system. After all, that is my point. Make this material your own though, and adjust it as you grow, change, and evolve.

In the next several chapters we will discuss the various guides that are our spirit associates. Reading about them before executing the above ritual would be good to do but is not necessary. You may want to review the earlier exercise and this template before continuing, or at least grab a top up for your tea or coffee.

Chapter Three: Your Master Teacher Guide

Let's start in the back of the circle with the master teacher guide. The master teacher guide is located directly behind you, and this is an excellent metaphor for their role in our life. This is the first guide that someone usually makes contact with, as it is the predominant guide for most people. Usually, if people only work with one guide, this is the one. To determine who your master teacher guide is, ponder these questions from throughout your life. Many times, the master teacher guide is the invisible friend that children are commonly known to have. Yes, sometimes that invisible friend is a ghost, but more often than not it is our master teaching guide, keeping us company and developing a strong relationship with us in our receptive years that can grow over time. As we grow and develop, our receptivity to spirits of all kinds diminishes, unless we go out of our way to keep it alive and strong. This is why so many people that had invisible friends when they were younger, may not have much, if any, spirit contact in their adult years. Part of this is due to the biological changes we go through as we age, but part of it also has to do with the programming and conditioning we get through school and other social functions.

Exercise Two: To resume the exercises, think back to your youth. Did you have an imaginary friend? Many people I know had at least one, and usually more than that, but I do know a decent number of people that had no invisible friend when they were young, so keep this in mind when you start to talk to others about this. Usually each person has one main invisible friend, and if you fit that category, then you have already met your master teacher guide. You get bonus points if you still remember their name! But, if you didn't have an imaginary friend that is okay too, and really doesn't mean much. This is because we are given what we can handle in situations like this, so while some children may be okay with an invisible friend, others may not be, for a variety of reasons. These reasons may not all have to do with the child either. Let's say you were a creative child raised in an uncreative environment. Your master teacher guide might not have revealed itself to you because it could make your living situation worse. Or, it could cause you to work with it more than is healthy. Just because you didn't have an invisible childhood friend does not mean you don't have a master teacher guide, just so we're clear.

Has there ever been a time when you listened to that little voice in your head when making an important decision, and you turned out to make the correct decision when all was said and done? This is particularly true if you know in your core that it was not your own inner dialogue. This is another way that your master teacher guide can manifest in daily life that is subtle yet effective. A key here to discerning it is to make sure, as mentioned above, that it is not your inner dialogue, rationalizing a decision. This is also not your intuition telling you about something. When you hear this voice, it seems like it is guiding you to make the right decision. Yes, this could be seen as the next exercise. Think of your life and if this has been true for you at any time. If you have had that kind of experience, then know that it was your master teacher guide communicating with you in a way that you would receive. Secondly, have you ever felt like your life started improving when you started listening to this voice?

Have you ever scraped by in life by the skin of your teeth and felt like it was because someone or something special was looking out for you? While a lot of people may think this is God, or a god or goddess that they work with, this overlighting essence could just as easily (and it's usually the case) be your master teacher guide. This has been the case for me on more than one occasion. This does not mean that divinity does not intervene in your life, but rather, if you are not particularly spiritual or religious, this was simply a time when your master teacher guide had your back, so to speak, which leads us to something else to be briefly discussed. Our spirit guides are looking out for our best interests. We are a team in life. Yes, this also means that if you think your master teacher is leading you astray, it is probably not your master teacher guide. It is probably some other spirit that has taken a liking to you. And, if that voice was guiding you in a negative direction, it is probably a malicious spirit. I discuss all of this in depth in my book "Spirit Relations." Know though, that your master teacher guide will always do its best to guide you on the path to success in your life. Now, whether or not we receive or understand the message, that is another story. Your master teacher guide will do it's best to reach you though, for your greatest growth and good. After all, your success is its success, so there is no reason to lead you astray. Because of the karmic connections we discussed above, as we grow and succeed, so do they. Ponder these thoughts as the next exercise.

When certain important transitional phases of your life have been occurring, have you ever noticed a pattern of a certain being showing itself? This is kind of a tricky point, so let's clarify it. This is not referencing a particular deity showing up in your life during these times. For example, if you get images associated with the Egyptian goddess Isis during every transitional stage of your life, then it is Isis appearing, and not your master teacher guide. You master teacher guide will use different symbolism. If you have already set up a sacred symbol between you two, like we discussed in chapter two, then you already know what symbol to expect. But if you have not done that yet, this message can take on a different form. Let's say that during each transitional period in your life, you oddly see the silhouette of a man wearing a top hat in various places. This is probably a sign from your master teacher guide, telling you they are around you while you go through things. You can also see that this symbol will vary from person to person. Usually, this is something that is seen in a place that is out of the ordinary. To continue the example of the silhouette of the man, if you saw that image in a department store window, that's one thing. But if you see that image while walking down the sidewalk with no one around, then that is another thing. You do have to be careful with this point though, because sometimes what you are seeing is a non-guide spirit that is trying to make contact. I have found that is only true for those that already have a history of working with spirits, rather than for someone that is newly unfolding, so keep that in mind as you go through your development in this book. This would be the next exercise to ponder. Keep in mind though, that all of these points we are discussing here do not have to be present. In other words, you may find that some of these points are present in your life, and some are not. You do not have to check off each of these like marking a checklist. And, following that line of logic through, while I am sharing common patterns here, you may also notice different patterns that occur in your life that lead you to the same end of recognizing your master teacher guide. All of these points are simply based on my experiences, and there are many others out there with their own experiences that are more applicable to them.

If you answered yes to any of these, and/or the majority of these, then you have met your master teacher guide. The master teacher guide can best be understood as just that: your teacher. This is the guide that can help with the learning process that goes with an incarnated existence. Thus, it is primarily responsible for the spiritual learning that we go through while in form. It may not teach us the ins and outs of society, but it can help us in extrapolating the spiritual lessons and principles behind societal institutions and experiences. This also means that when we communicate with them, it would be wise to work with such measures of time and space as we understand them rather than in terms of how they understand them. Time works differently over there, so concepts like "soon" may not be that soon in our understanding of time. This means that when we do guide work, we should be specific when necessary for clarification. But this also means we should carefully pick and choose what we converse with them about. Because they are more of a spiritual nature, asking them for mundane things is not really their strength or focus. Asking them whether or not you should go on a particular diet plan is not encouraged, but rather asking them to guide you to the right people, person, or information source to make an informed, healthy decision, would be the way to go. I like to address this point quite a bit when I work with my guides. If I am asking my master teacher guide about the timing of something, I don't settle for a generic answer like "soon" or "later." I ask for specifics. This is good for accountability, as well as accuracy and building trust. Yes, we can hold our spirit guides accountable, just like they can hold us accountable. They hold us accountable by working with us only insofar as we work with them, and only as we work with them, speaking to us on our level. This is something that is not discussed a lot in books on spirit guides. Like us, they are subjected to karmic laws just like we are. This means they can incur karma through their interactions with us, just like we can incur karma in our interactions with them. It goes both ways, and the important takeaway from this is that they are not above any sort of morality or universal laws. Like us, they deal with the consequences of this relationship. Take a moment to review this material before moving on with the rest of the chapter, because we are now going to explore some tangents for the sake of clarification and completeness. First, let's start with a common notion.

Your Master Teacher is NOT your Holy Guardian Angel

There, I said it. I don't regret it, but I also realize a lot of people do not share this view, so allow me to clarify. Not everyone works with the idea of a holy guardian angel, for starters, but if you do, let's delineate some things. As metaphysics teaches us, angels are from the devic kingdom, which is also the same kingdom as fairies and other etheric beings. The use of the word kingdom here is in line with the other commonly found scientific kingdoms, so in the Western Esoteric Tradition, we have the animal kingdom, the human kingdom, the plant kingdom, the devic kingdom, and the rock and mineral kingdom. Everything that lives falls into one of these categories. Our four main spirit guides, while non-physical, were human at one time. They went through a human life like we are doing. This can be seen as true because in order for them to guide us, they have to have experience with things that we will encounter, and in order to have those experiences, they had to have had form. Angels have never been incarnated as physical humans.

In some books about spirit guides, the word angels is used instead. Some would say this is a difference of beliefs, and if that is your case, then continue to use the word angels to describe them. While I am sharing strong opinions here, I also realize that these are not facts to many people, and that many of us have different beliefs. In my spiritual paradigm, the holy guardian angel is a different being entirely. First, it is from a different kingdom, as you just read. Secondly, it is an external being, and while the master teacher guide can also be seen as an external being, the holy guardian angel is even more external than that. For example, you may see your holy guardian angel, but to see your master teacher guide (other than clairvoyantly) is quite rare.

Then there is the point to consider that to many people, the holy guardian angel was appointed to us, whereas the master teacher guide is one that we enter into a relationship with on even footing, more like a contract like we discussed in chapter two. Usually that is not the case when it comes to your holy guardian angel. Some people believe the holy guardian angel is assigned to us from God, but to others, this holy guardian angel is assigned to us through an astrological connection. In either case, you can see how this differs from the master teacher guide. However you view this subject, it would be wise to get it straight in your head before continuing your spirit guide work. You can align with what I said or not, it really doesn't matter, but at least think this concept through before getting too far involved with your spirit associates.

A Past Life?

It is also worth noting that our master teacher guide is not us from a past life. This is a common misconception that does require some addressing here. Once we drop the body of that previous life, our identity self, also known as our personality self, ceases to exist, and the experiences and lessons we had, come back to our soul in order to be addressed and integrated. Sometimes that personality self is so strong that it stays on the astral plane as a hollow, empty shell. This is kept alive by the memories of those that knew it, so over time, yes, it does fade. Sometimes it takes years, while other times it takes decades or even centuries. It is a shell because its soul has left. Technically, *your* soul has left, reunited with the part of it that is beyond the confines of one life. The ego of that particular lifetime did not leave, though. It grew attached to physical form, and to existing in general.

We may think that shell is our master teacher guide because of our comfort in its presence, and its familiarity. After all, we were it at one time, but it has nothing to teach us beyond what it experienced while in physical form and existence. This makes it more limited than our master teacher guide. There is also the fact that times change, so the environment it was in is most likely highly outdated, culturally and socially, if nothing else. When you stop and ponder this, you see a process that is illustrated. The soul sends down a personality during an incarnation. When that lifetime is done, the soul ascends with the knowledge it garnered through those experiences. However, the personality-self, if it developed a strong will, developed a desire to continue to exist, but since the soul that inhabited it has left, it is simply going through the process of trying to continue to exist. But eventually, time swallows all, and it dissipates. There are many factors that go into this, but you see the pattern. Meanwhile, the soul is either exploring or learning on the other side of the veil, or it has already come back down into physical form for its next life. The moral of the story is to be careful when first exploring your relationship with your master teacher guide, as you do not want to make this mistake. There is a lot of esoteric material out there that discusses this, but I will stop this tangent for now to keep things focused on guide work. Just know that this exists, though, and beware of it when you or loved ones are opening up to guide work.

Is Your Master Teacher Guide, God?

This is another interesting perspective to ponder. A thought I have had many times, that I have heard echoed by others, is that the religious instances in the past of hearing "God's voice" were actually communication between a person and their Master Teacher Guide. A tangent of this is that the discarnate entity was actually the person's holy guardian angel, instead of God.

We will not go into this too deeply, because bluntly, there's not a lot of depth to the conversation. It is entirely possible that all of those examples through history (Most of them coming from the Bible, i.e. Abraham hearing God telling him to commit murder.) were not examples of a person communicating with God, but rather their holy guardian angel or master teacher guide. Personally, this situation looks to me like an interaction between a person and their holy guardian angel or master teacher guide, but other people may have other perspectives. On one hand, this is another example of just having this clear in your own mind before continuing the work in here. On the other hand, this is also a reminder to know the signs of spirit contact vs communing within yourself. Legitimate spirit contact will have external manifestations, whereas inner communion, especially with guides, generally will not. You will actually feel a presence of a spirit in the room if your spirit contact is quality. Or, you will have some sort of other physical manifestation to demonstrate the spirit's presence. So, to illustrate, Moses and the burning bush could be considered legitimate spirit contact because of the external nature of the burning bush (unless he was on psychedelics), whereas the above example of Abraham's voice would be more akin to internal spirit contact.

Think about this for a minute though. Think of how much your perspective on religion and spirituality would change if you meticulously went through your sacred texts and applied this critical thinking tool. Re-addressing these things would significantly change your spiritual paradigm, and most likely many other things. It definitely changes the story of Abraham, because now we see that it was not God that told Abraham to do it, it could have been his master teacher guide, which greatly takes away from the legitimacy of that entire situation. And, it opens the door for other interpretations of those events.

The takeaway from this section is simply that through history, and still occurring today, people are thinking they are hearing God, when in reality they are hearing the voice of their guide. This is something to ponder, and while I have shared my preferred perspective on it, I also understand this is highly subjective and largely faith driven, so come to your own conclusions. If this is your first exposure to these themes, then consider what I say, but ultimately decide for yourself. There is also the point to consider that these two ideas are not mutually exclusive. Maybe sometimes you are hearing your guide, but others you are actually hearing the voice of a god. That is entirely possible, too, but to be able to spot the difference requires experience, education, and training.

Then What is It?

Ahh, the eternal question. How do you categorize your master teacher guide? Is there even a need for categorization? One of the ways that the human mind works is through categorization, so it is only natural to think about categorizing it, and then to do so if you feel inclined. There is nothing wrong with wanting to categorize it. You don't have to do that though if you don't want. I enjoy this mental exercise, but that is just me. At the end of the day, there is really not much I can say on this point because, if you want to know who or what it is, ask it! Go straight to the source. If you think "Oh, I don't know how to do that," finish reading this book, and if you need further clarification, then consult my book "Spirit Relations." If you doubt your skill, then like a musician or an athlete, practice, practice, practice. If you believe something about it now, and five years from now your mind changes, that is okay. Change is the only constant, and it is healthy to revisit things the older you get.

I will share my experiences with you to give you some ideas and direction. When it comes to my master teacher guide, I know his name. I know a lot about his life. I understand our connection not just in the present, but also in the context of the past and the future, and I have a sense of his essential being. We have a symbol established between the two of us that I see when he wants to communicate with me, or that I can use to communicate with him, and that's about the totality of it. Whereas, when it comes to my holy guardian angel, I know different things, and really more things. This does set us off on another tangent again though, which is that your master teacher guide may or may not be the same gender or gender identity as you. Some people think if you are a guy, your master teacher guide will be a guy, too, but that is not always the case. This is important to keep in mind when first beginning. On a technical point, your master teacher guide does not have a gender or gender identity, but they will show one to us to better facilitate spirit contact. This may or may not change through the course of your relationship with it, or over the course of your life. Some people even think that their master teacher guide should appear as their romantic soul mate, but again, that is not always the case, so if it is not there, it would be wise to avoid seeking it out.

Some people have made the case for it to be a created thoughtform, but this is not the case, either. For those of you that don't know, a thoughtform is a created consciousness that is brought about through focused energy on a particular topic. The more you think about something, the more energy you invest in it, the more this happens, the more sentient it becomes. The more sentient it becomes, the more consciousness it develops, the more consciousness it develops, the more it wants to live and thrive. The theory basically goes like this: By being introduced to guides, you start to think about them, and the more you think about them and work with them using various techniques, the more you build up energy around them, and the more that occurs, the more the thoughtform is built. I do see the logic with this, but let's look at a counterpoint. This only works on a conscious level if you know what you are doing. Yes, the process of building a thoughtform can be done unconsciously, but what we're talking about here is a complex level of consciousness. Usually, unless they have been around for a long, long, time (such as in the case of gods and goddesses), the level of consciousness for thoughtforms like this is not as advanced or complex as what you will encounter when you start doing deep guide work. When you are first making contact with your master teacher guide, it is true that it may seem like a thoughtform because all you are doing is establishing a way to communicate, as well as other identifying features. Once the actual exchange of information happens, and wisdom is revealed through meditation and communication, you will discover it is a more complex and deeper level of consciousness that you are dealing with, rather than what would be present if you were interacting with a standard thoughtform. This is also a good rule of thumb to use when you are interacting with spirits and discarnate entities in general.

Where Is It From?

This may seem like an odd topic, and possibly even unnecessary, but it does deserve a brief divergence. It is not necessary to know where your master teacher guide is from, but by addressing the key things we will discuss, you will be in a position to have a more open mind that can help you not only with guide work, but spiritual unfoldment in general. Technically, usually, no one will learn the exact origin of their master teacher guide, and that is okay. I do not know where mine is from, for example. I do know where many of my past lives occurred, yes, but as to the details of my master teacher guide, I have no idea, nor do I have the desire to learn them, either.

Having said that, why is this section here, then? It is here for one important reason. The reason this section is here is to remind you that your master teacher guide may not be from this dimension. Remember that on the other side of the veil, time and space do not exist, which means it is entirely possible that your master teacher guide is from a different dimension. Yes, this also implies that perhaps your soul has spent some time in a different dimension during the course of its development, too. That, however, is a conversation for another time.

While other dimensions may seem like something relegated to the realm of science fiction and fantasy, more and more scientific evidence is mounting that these really do exist. The universe (or multiverse as I like to call it) is comprised of many different dimensions, and one only has to look as far as quantum physics to see this discussion. Science and modern spirituality are blending on this singularity point, and because of this, more and more deeper crossover subjects are being addressed in a new light. At the current evolutionary point of our human brains we are not at a place where we can clearly recall past-lives, let alone lives in other dimensions, but when we are in our pure form of spirit such safety trappings of forgetfulness and hierarchical consciousness are not present, and our soul is free to explore wherever and whenever we want, for as long as we want. This does mean that we can make connections with beings from other dimensions, and yes, following that line of logic through, some of these beings may become our guides in various capacities. This opens the door to a lot of possibilities, doesn't it?

I put this piece in here to give you confidence as you develop your relationships with all of your guides, and specifically your master teacher guide. If you begin communicating with it, and it shows an appearance that is peaceful but alien, that is quite okay. If it initially uses a language that you don't recognize, it may be a language from that other dimension. The good news is that it will adjust to you when it comes to communication and language. Yes, it is bound by your limitations of language, but it is in a position to adapt to you when using language to communicate. You may also find that its appearance changes to appeal to your comfort level, as mentioned earlier.

Speaking of language, and this is true of all guide work, usually your guides will communicate to you using symbols and symbolism rather than words. In order to use words, spirit associates *really* have to lower their energy and vibration to make it happen. They operate in a different realm than we do. It is a finer place that largely operates through one's subconscious, and the subconscious deals more in symbols than words. In some ways, this is a red flag. If you are dealing with spirits that only use language, then you are not dealing with higher vibrational beings. If you are dealing with spirits that use symbols, then you are connecting with spirits of a like and higher vibration. If the spirits you deal with use both symbols and language, then you know you are on the right path, because it knows how to adapt to where you are at on your path, and after all, it is the more adaptable of the species that survives and evolves.

Yes, it is common to not know where your master teacher guide is from, but when pondering this point, you would be wise to open your mind to the fact that there is more than one dimension, so it stands to reason that your master teacher guide may be from one of a number of dimensions. But then again, this also means that perhaps your soul is from one of those other dimensions too, but that is a topic for another time. For now, just be open to the idea in the name of preparing yourself for what you might see and experience in your spirit guide work. And, bluntly, you can also feel free to ignore this tangent, but a book on the guide experience would not be complete without a brief discussion of this topic. I have known many people over the years that did not consider this when starting out, so they were left bewildered when their master teacher guide appeared to them in an alien image, or on an alien landscape. This is the doubt I would like to save from you. When you are first interacting with your guides, keep as open of a mind as possible when it comes to interpreting the information received. Be mindful though, that your success is its success.

Chapter Four: Your Gatekeeper Guide

The gatekeeper guide is also sometimes known as the guardian guide, and its role is just that: to guard us. This guide stands out in front of us, and hence its role is clarified. Often times this is a Native American guide according to traditional Spiritualism, but this is not necessarily 100% true. When meeting and working with your gatekeeper guide, it is wise to pay attention to how they are equipped, for these implements give you insight into how they protect you. For example, if they have a dagger or sword, then they use the tools of the mental plane and the mind. But if they have a wand or a staff, then they use willpower and the spiritual plane to assist in your defense. Sometimes gatekeeper guides have no equipment, and that is fine, too. This simply tells us that one of the ways they protect us is through skill and cunning, honesty and transparency. This isn't an absolute, though, so the sliding scale of grey should be considered when dealing with them.

When dealing with this particular guide, I like to recall the story of Ra's solar barque (boat) from ancient Egypt, briefly mentioned earlier. As Ra the sun god, traveled daily across the sky, he encountered many threats to his existence. The retinue of gods on the barque, including Ra himself, were protected by the god Set who went out in front of the group, slaying the enemies of Ra to protect the gods in the barque. Using this imagery is my personal preference, but I share it here because it shows a creative way you can use your imagination when executing visualization techniques. If we put this into context of traditional Spiritualism, we also see something rather profound. The Rashid Stone (Commonly called the Rosetta

Stone), which gave us the key to translating ancient Egyptian hieroglyphics, was discovered in 1799, approximately forty-nine years before Spiritualism the religion was begun. This means that all things related to Egyptology were still in their infancies, and even more infantile would have been the exposure of this monumentous find to the average person, which would include the Fox sisters. Even if they did know what was available about Egypt, the story of Ra's voyage is less likely to have been known. Metaphysically this parallel could be interpreted as proving the validity of the placement of the gatekeeper guide. Some people would say this is speculation, but I share it here to stimulate your mind to consider the energetic connections that span thousands of years. This could show validity because it shows that since time immemorial, the idea of a protector going out in front, has been around.

There are two strong roles that the gatekeeper guide fulfills in our lives. The first role is that of the guardian as mentioned above. The second role is that it acts like a guardian against other spirits that may have an unwholesome agenda against us, and in this way it is often times said that the gatekeeper is more active on the other side of the veil than on this one. Because of this, sometimes they do a lot of work without us knowing about it. One of the ways that we can bring our consciousness into alignment with what they're doing is to study universal, karmic, and spiritual laws so that we have an idea of what they're facing. While this might not give us 100% knowledge of what they are doing, it can definitely help us to better grasp the gravity of the situations that they face.

This does mean that they not only protect us in the spiritual world, but also the physical. We should be careful not to see this as an absolute, though. After all, our gatekeeper guide can only physically protect us inasmuch as we protect ourselves and make intelligent choices. If we find that we are constantly putting ourselves in harm's way, then it should be no surprise if we get harmed once in a while. There is only so much any guide can do to help us, particularly if we don't help ourselves. To illustrate, if we are constantly putting ourselves in danger, then the law of averages will catch up to us eventually, and we will suffer consequences based on our actions, regardless of how much our Gatekeeper Guide works on protecting us.

A tangent of this is that sometimes we will receive blessings in disguise from our Gatekeeper Guide. For example, this guide may protect us by having our car break down so that we are not on the road at a certain time when we would otherwise get into an accident. This stresses the importance of being open minded and interpreting messages and circumstances correctly, rather than what we *think* is correct. Part of this can be solved through humility, while part of it can be solved through meditation. Another way that our gatekeeper guide can protect us is through changing what could have been a major incident into a minor one. For example, if we are in a dangerous situation, and we get out of it with a stubbed toe rather than a broken leg. To the cynic, this would be a failure of the gatekeeper guide, but in reality, this was the best the guide could do, given the circumstances. In this case, it is all about context and gratitude.

Appearance

Yes, in traditional Spiritualism, especially in the early days of it, your gatekeeper guide was usually seen as a Native American. This needs context though, as I have found gatekeeper guides of myself and others to not be Native American, so some explanation is required. The time period of the rise and true growth of Spiritualism was up through the 1920s. In America, the USA as we know it today was still being formed, and one of the ways this was occurring was through the subjugation, murder, and imprisonment of Native American tribes. Regardless of how the rest of the world viewed all of this turmoil, the fact is that Native Americans were seen as exotic, sometimes brutal, savages, but also contained in their communities was a profound sense of spirituality. Their naturalistic views of a living spirituality were quite the injections into otherwise centuries old and rigid beliefs This, along with the French Occult Revival, and English developments of magick, were fueling a spiritual renaissance. In many cases, Native Americans were part of circus acts that traveled to other parts of the world. While this is barbaric and horrific to consider, not everyone in the audiences saw these traits in the foreigners. One thing that was for sure was that they were exotic, and to the enlightened, quite spiritual and persecuted.

Another piece of information for context is that they were being killed by the thousands, if not millions. Metaphysically, this means a lot of their spirits were going across the veil into the spirit world, more so than were being born into the physical world. Their deep spirituality also meant that they were generally stronger in nature, with a strong honor code. So, it is commonly believed that many of them stayed on the other side of the veil and chose to become spirit guides for those that were open to it.

In a lot of ways, this is a major root of new world spirituality as it exists today. Native American spiritual teachings have had a profound influence on modern spirituality over the last century or so, and this does not exist as readily in the old world. There are many reasons for this, but it is worth pointing out, because it is one of the differentiating factors between the two worlds.

Over the last twenty years, I have not seen Native Americans being gatekeeper guides to be true on average. Yes, I do know and have met many with Native American guides, and specifically gatekeeper guides, but I have observed this is more of a generational trait, and even that bold statement needs some clarification. The demographic I have seen this trait most common in is the generation commonly called the "Baby Boomers." Younger generations have a more colorful spin on this classic Spiritualism teaching. I have known many, many people not in that demographic that have dragons for guardian guides, or even various deities from global civilizations, such as the ancient Egyptian and Norse. Part of this common appearance was discussed earlier in the book, but the part that hasn't been that is applicable here is the fact that Native Americans are no longer considered as exotic as they were. Part of their exoticism two centuries ago was the fact that they were largely a mystery. Now, a plethora of books exist defining their various spiritual beliefs and systems. In addition to books, there are many websites that exist to clarify them. And, bluntly, Native Americans themselves and their descendants are around, and many are educators and disseminators of information. Because of the internet and other pieces of modern technology, more accurate information can be shared, a trait which was not present twenty-five years ago, let alone one hundred years ago.

Native American spirituality can also usually be broken down by tribe, and what is being exposed is that something that was once seen as nebulous (Native American beliefs) is now being looked at in a more microscopic way (Cherokee beliefs, vs Iroquois vs Blackfoot, etc). In other words, information is now readily available. The Baby Boomers were the last generation to really be at the threshold of the transition from pre-industrial revolution ways to post-industrial revolution ways, and because of this, traditional Spiritualism continued along as it always did. Information is more readily available, and in a lot of ways, there has been a liberal expansion when it comes to living and practicing spirituality in the twenty-first century. This has led to the above observation from what I can tell, but remember that in situations like this, there are no absolutes. I'm sure there are many non-Baby Boomers out there that have Native American gatekeeper guides, and I am sure that there are many Baby Boomers out there that have non-Native American gatekeeper guides. For myself, personally, my gatekeeper guide is not Native American. He is an indigenous person, just not from the Americas.

I touched on this earlier in the master teacher guide section, but I want to further clarify it here as it applies to all guides. There is no gender or gender identity implicit in spirit guides. In other words, just because you have a gatekeeper guide does not mean it has to be a man, or a woman for that case. Remember that we are talking about functions for various guides, but this is in context of where you are at in your personal and spiritual growth and development. I reiterate, they will appear however is best for you and the development you two share. Remember too, that their appearance may change over time for various reasons, so they may start off as extremely masculine or feminine, and years later, they may change to the opposite. All of this occurs between the two of you, and really, it is no one's business but your own. Staying silent about your spirit guides and connection to them can be quite valuable. This does not mean it is of a secret nature, but rather use your own discretion when it comes to who you talk to about these deeply personal relationships and subjects. Gender, and gender identity of spirit guides is aligned to you and is an intimate connection that can reveal a lot not only about who you are, but also where you are going.

When it comes to accessories, this is highly subjective as well. Many times they are seen as being armed with vicious weapons, or having a savage and disturbing appearance. In a lot of ways, this parallels the idea from the classic "beauty and the beast" tale, where the being that looks like a beast is actually quite nice and oftentimes gentle. Well, they are at least that way to you. When they do their duty though, they may behave as terrible as their countenance. It is possible that they do not have any accessories, either. When we put this together with what has been discussed in this section, yes, we arrive at the conclusion that really, anything is possible, so when you communicate with your gatekeeper guide, just have an open mind and ask yourself what your gatekeeper guide tells you about yourself.

Behavior

This will be a small section because there is not a lot to say, as so much of it is subjective. That is the point of this section, though, to illustrate that there is no right or wrong way this guide, or any others, for that matter, will behave. With the three other main spirit guides, their roles are clearly defined, and this implies that they will communicate with us on a regular basis. After all, our Doctor of Philosophy guide can only give us so much insight and information through non-verbal communication, as an example. Yes, it can use symbolism, which is deeper and more profound, but there will still be those regular times that it will communicate telepathically, if nothing else. None of these are the cases with the gatekeeper guide.

Really, the gatekeeper guide does not have to communicate. It simply protects us. It can and does communicate though, but I have found this to be rare. The way it communicates is by simply giving us insight and direction as to what to do and how to do it in order to help us avoid being in a position of danger. So for example, you may get a message from it saying "don't go in there," or "stop," but these will be brief messages, because they have to be brief due to the imminent threat. Usually, the gatekeeper guide will emphasize avoiding potentially hazardous situations rather than helping us when we are already in them. There are exceptions to this of course, but a lot of the role of the gatekeeper guide is being proactive, rather than reactive.

This means that we should really pay attention to this guide, because many of its messages will be subtle and immediate. I have heard many stories from people over the years that go like this: *I was taking my normal route home after work, when I heard my guide tell me to turn and go a different way. When I got home, I found out that there was an accident along my normal route, and if I had not turned, it would have been me!*

Conversely, I have heard the opposite variation of this, in that the person does not listen to their gatekeeper guide, and they get into an accident because of it. For some, this was a wake-up call to more attentively listen to their guides, but for others, they did not translate it this way. This is a typical example of the relationship between a gatekeeper guide and an individual. While I use the distinct example of an accident to illustrate the point here, sometimes what the gatekeeper guide protects us from is something more cerebral, or emotionally or mentally damaging, so let's turn our attention to that.

Sometimes our gatekeeper guide will intervene when we might otherwise get exposed to damaging or incendiary information. A good example of this could be why you are not able to attend school or church when a particular topic is being discussed. In these cases, it is not so much that something physically bad might happen, but rather that the ideas conveyed there at that time may be psychologically damaging. It could be that you recently had an emotional upheaval in your life, and the subject being discussed would trigger those painful memories, which could, in turn, retard your progress and growth. You can see how this is equally applicable in many life areas. This could be true in the professional, religious, personal, or any combination of these, life areas. I am sure we have all heard stories of the people that were running late, which was unlike them, and because of that, their life was spared from some tragedy. These are examples that can be studied in order to learn more about our gatekeeper guide.

Remember though, that keeping yourself safe is not solely the gatekeeper guide's responsibility. Let's be practical for a moment and admit that keeping ourselves safe is our responsibility first and foremost. Personal responsibility and accountability should be first and foremost before any guide work is attempted. And the more you focus on physical plane safety, the more your gatekeeper guide can help you. This is because, as discussed earlier, our guides can only help us as much as we know about a particular subject. Thus, the more we know and learn, the more tools we have in our toolbox, and thus the bigger the artistic palette a particular guide has to use when it comes to communicating with us. To quote an Islamic proverb, "trust in Allah, but tie up your camel." In other words, yes, have faith, but do your part as well. If your life is such that your gatekeeper guide works overtime, you may want to consider making changes in your life to make you safer and more secure in general. To do this, you may have to learn about self-defense and personal safety, and as you learn these subjects, your gatekeeper guide gets put into a better position to help you when you need it on the spot throughout life.

I share all of this because there have been a few times in my life I have met someone that relied on their gatekeeper guide to bail them out of every dangerous situation they were in, which means of course that they were constantly playing the victim card. Eventually, as is the case a lot of the times, the gatekeeper guide quit responding. This was a wakeup call for the individual, and this is also completely in line with what I discussed earlier, about the nature of the karmic relationship between us and our guides. We are linked karmically, but if something like this occurs, the spirit guide is well within their rights to step back or leave altogether. This may seem like shocking news, but really it is just an example of cause and effect but playing out between the physical and spiritual planes. Shirking your responsibility to yourself and expecting your spirit guides to pick up the slack are two of the spiritually worst things you can do when it comes to guide work. Metaphysically, you are stunting your own growth to the point that you will probably have to repeat this lifetime, and maybe one or two others. Our spirit guides are not pets for us to train, nor are they beneath us in any way, shape, or form. I have found the best way to interact with them is to treat your relationship with them like you would treat other relationships in your life, respectfully and conscientiously.

The hidden morality here, which is true with all guides, but especially obvious when it comes to the gatekeeper guide, is that it is wise to stay humble. When interacting with the gatekeeper guide, you do have to put your own ego aside to a large degree and surrender to trusting the guide when it communicates. In the above example, if you heard your gatekeeper guide tell you to take an alternate route home, but you thought to yourself "Nah, nothing EVER happens on that street," and then you got into an accident because you ignored them, you have just lived out an example of the danger and toxicity of hubris, also known as pride. Pride can be so damaging in situations like this. When dealing with your gatekeeper guide, it is wise to simply assume that in dangerous situations, they probably know more than you do. Really, this is common sense. Because they are in the spirit world, their senses are attuned to different frequencies than ours are, and most times, they are attuned to more frequencies at that! Many times I have listened to my gatekeeper guide in situations like the ones discussed above, and not only did I not understand why my guide led me that way, I also saw no visible results that I missed or experienced. This did not stop me from listening to them though, because I am pretty sure that as soon as I did, something would happen, as Murphy has declared and clarified over and over.

I have found that most times, the gatekeeper guide is the strong, silent type. I have not known them to communicate much, and when they do, it is usually brief. Each element in the Western Esoteric Tradition can reflect a particular communication style. This is something that is discussed a lot in astrology, but outside of that, it is not generally addressed. Here are the general rules of thumb to follow that you can use not just for your guide work, but also when it comes to learning about communication styles and how they are handled in modern spirituality. Earth heavy emphasis generally means silence more than speech, and when communicating, words are calculated and methodical. Water heavy emphasis means the amount of conversation is based on emotions, and the communication style is that of manipulating or expressing emotions. Air heavy emphasis generally denotes one that communicates a lot, but also has a fantastic way with words. The subject material may also be more cerebral than physical. Finally, fire heavy emphasis generally denotes speaking with passion in short, controlled bursts. If you apply this line of thinking to the elemental correspondences of your guides, you can see what to expect before you start working with them.

Exercise Three: Using the Spirit Guide Contact Template from chapter two, contact your Gatekeeper Guide, and record your results in your journal. Remember to pay attention to unspoken details.

Chapter Five: Your Doctor of Philosophy Guide

This guide is positioned on our right side in traditional Spiritualism, and this subtle placement gives us a lot of insight into their role in our lives. The Doctor of Philosophy is the one that assists us with mental and spiritual development through the use of critical thinking skills and understanding. This is the guide that assists us when we connect the dots with pieces of information that we encounter throughout our growth and evolution. This is the guide that can also cause profound epiphanies and realizations when it comes to spiritual breakthroughs, or the discovery of previously unknown skills. When this guide is worked with, emotions become secondary to clear, analytical thought. The intuition technically falls in line with cognitive thinking here, but as we'll see when we address the next guide, the intuition is something that is handled by a different guide. This overlap is something to pay attention to, though, as the concept of overlapping is something that is true of all of our primary guides, regardless of their role. For example, sometimes we learn the philosophy of defense from our gatekeeper guide, to illustrate the point. This does not mean that our Doctor of Philosophy guide is knowledgeable of all religions and philosophies out there, but rather the ones that are most in line with our spiritual background and tapestry. This is the guide that assists us in getting us where we need to be, spiritually speaking, and does so through promulgating thought processes.

Spirit guides are not absolute, which means that overlapping between guides is common. This is an important point to keep in mind when you are cultivating your relationships with them. As illustrated above, one guide may teach you the principles of something, but another guide may show you how to put those principles into action. It is easy to fall into the trap of exclusivity, but I encourage you to be wary of this as you execute your work. The only thing to really pay attention to here is that of accidentally thinking that all guides can do all things. In a lot of ways, this is the pendulum swinging to the opposite end of the spectrum. On one end is the absolute mentality, the belief that guides do not and cannot overlap, and on the other end of the spectrum is the belief that if guides overlap, there is no such thing as specialties when it comes to guides. Both perspectives are incorrect, and as with most things in life, the truth lies somewhere in the middle. Even that middle, fulcrum point, is subjective to the individual, so even that should be taken with a grain of salt.

The Doctor of Philosophy guide is one that can assist us, not think for us, and this is something that is wise to remember when dealing with all of our guides. They are an enhancement rather than a crutch to be used. They are also not karmic scapegoats due to the fact that we live in a free will zone, and are thus responsible for our own decisions, actions, and consequences thereof. This guide can be heard the clearest when we are mentally at our clearest, and thus it is always wise to still the mind in order to receive the teachings that come from this guide. This also means that one of the ways you can put yourself in a position to better work with this guide is by cultivating practices that have to do with clarity of thought. This is more than just using logic on a regular basis. This also includes physical activities that promote brain health and cognitive thinking. For example, physical exercise, especially cardiovascular exercise, is something that has been proven to promote clear thinking. Mental exercises, such as crossword puzzles and other brain teasers, can also be done to keep your mind clear of unwanted and detrimental influences.

Even though the following point applies to all guides, I include it in this section because we are currently discussing the guide that most has to do with the mental plane and the mind. This point is that of the necessity of diet, and how that impacts our guide work. This point has been well-documented in metaphysical circles for many years now, so there is ample material available for those of you that may want to explore this point further. While some of this may seem "out there," all of it is actually rooted in long-standing traditional teachings of occultism. Each guide corresponds to one of the four elements in the Western Esoteric Tradition - earth, air, fire, and water, and each of those elements have psychospiritual traits attached to them. But, it should never be forgotten that there is a physical side of these traits as well. While that is common sense based on the elements, we are going to look at the tangible manifestation of them in a personal way, and this can help you deeper your connection with your guides.

Let's break this down. Your gatekeeper guide is the guide of earth, because they protect you, both spiritually and physically. Therefore, if you want to deepen your connection with it, then doing physical exercises and other physical things would be wise to do. For example, if you want to improve your connection with your gatekeeper guide, then you could learn a self-defense practice, such as Jujitsu. But you could also eat foods that keep you grounded, such as meat and grains. Any food that puts you back in your body would fall under this category, so it is not as stringent or specific as I might make it look here. Your Doctor of Chemistry guide aligns with the element of water, which tells us that if you want to deepen your connection to it, it would be wise to increase your water intake. You could extrapolate this to include drinking smoothies instead of eating full, seven course meals. By default, this also means it would be wise to avoid drinking harmful substances, such as sodas with high fructose corn syrup and other potentially toxic substances. Yes, this could also extend into a public service announcement of the dangers of alcohol, but I think just mentioning it here is enough to drive that point home. In traditional Spiritualism, especially at the tail end of the nineteenth century, there was a very strict teaching about this. The teaching was, as I learned it in Spiritualism, simply that if you had ever taken a drink of alcohol in your life, you could NEVER become a medium through them. The common belief was that as soon as you did take that drink, it put a hole in your auric body that could never be repaired, and therefore your spirit work would always be damaged and fractured! That is not necessarily the case now, but it was true for many decades around the turn of the twentieth century. And having said this, I'm sure you can see why I was not taught as a traditional Spiritualist. Metaphysically, I understand the concept, but it leaves very little room for growth, healing, and a list of other, higher vibrational ideas.

Your Doctor of Philosophy guide correlates to the element of air, and one of the ways you can deepen your connection with it is through stretching exercises and improving the circulation of blood through your veins. Whether this is Yoga or some other form of stretching really doesn't matter. Although, if you are going to use Yoga to do this, then it would be wise to learn the spiritual dimension of Yoga in addition to all of the poses and other stretching exercises. Air is also breath, so breathing exercises are also good to use to this end. This can also be extended to include verbal magical practices, such as mantras and other chant-based techniques. On a fun tangent, this also means that singing is good to do to connect with this guide. Finally, your Master Teacher guide corresponds to the element of fire, and don't forget that fire has a double meaning for the purposes of our conversation here.

One meaning of fire is physical activity, but let's delineate this to separate it out from what was previously discussed about the element of earth. In this case, physical activity is more along the lines of putting in the work to achieve your results. So, to illustrate, if you want to deepen your connection with your Master Teacher guide, then you could walk your talk, so to speak, avoiding things like hypocrisy or hollow words. This should make it clear that what I'm referencing here is the age-old occult teaching of doing the work. Now it is clear what this has to do with, and how it is different from the traits of the gatekeeper guide previously discussed. Getting motivated and invested in your own success is what is highlighted here.

The other meaning of fire is that of spiritual fire, so let's turn our attention to that for further clarification. If you want to increase your connection with your Master Teacher Guide, then it is wise to deepen your spirituality, and if you do not feel like you have any spirituality, then it would be wise to simply begin! It is hard to have a connection with a spiritual being like this if you do not have a developed spiritual nature of yourself. This is more than just clarifying what you believe and why. This goes into the realm of your spiritual practices, and if you are just starting out with those, then it may take some time to find what works for you and what doesn't.

Here is an example to illustrate the point. I have known many people throughout my life that have been drawn to ceremonial magick, which is a specialized branch of ritual magick, but not all of them stick with it over the duration of their life. There are many reasons for this. For some, they couldn't do it because they had other responsibilities that took up so much of their time and energy that when they did their ceremonial magick practices, they were often exhausted, or felt like they were not getting out of it everything that they desired. Sometimes these responsibilities were in the form of child raising, and sometimes these were in the form of taking care of the elderly or the infirmed. For others, the reason was that they had to work multiple jobs just to make ends meet. I share all of these examples here to show that they had to walk away from ceremonial practices for legitimate reasons, and those reasons were not due to laziness.

Choosing a spiritual practice and regimen can be a little complicated because you have to find one that is in tune with your life and what you have to work with, rather than a practice you might desire. If you have an extremely active life, then a low maintenance daily practice might be wise to do, but if you have a life that includes lots of free time, then you have a little more flexibility and wiggle room to experiment with more aggressive practices. A key point to remember here is that there is no right or wrong amount of spiritual practices. For some people, simply having one thing that you do every day is enough, but for others, this might be too little. You are the final arbiter for this, so while it is good to get different thoughts and perspectives from other people, ultimately it is your choice, and you should not be denigrated for your choice. Keep in mind, also, that you can go back later and change it. If you find that one practice a day is too little, then feel free to add another practice, but if you do that, you might want to make it a small practice, just to be safe. You can always add more later anyway, so it's not like you are locked into anything. On a side note, corresponding guides to elements like this is something I have not seen discussed before, so if you arrive to conclusions beyond the scope of this book, please explore them. This line of thinking also means that you could align the four powers of the Sphinx to your guides, as well as the directional teachings of the Native American Medicine Wheel. Or, you could leave both of those out, it really doesn't matter. I simply offer all of this here as food for thought.

Philosophy?

When I was first learning Spiritualism, I really had to work through the idea that this guide is called the Doctor of Philosophy, because I have never really worked with or liked philosophy. I am a firm believer in a teaching from Aleister Crowley, "philosophy is the enemy of magick," so I had to rationalize working with a guide called the Doctor of Philosophy. This was easier done than said though, as it quickly became apparent to me that this guide is not so much about philosophy as it is the mental plane in general like we clarified above, and when Spiritualism was being developed, the term philosophy was as accurate as any to describe how they assist us. Knowing the etymology of the word 'philosophy' helped in developing an understanding of it. Also keep in mind that when Spiritualism was coming into being, the subject of psychology had not been invented yet, so a true, deep, modern understanding of the mind was still many decades off.

The word comes from two roots strung together: 'philo,' which essentially means 'love,' and 'soph,' derived from 'sophia,' which means 'wisdom.' So technically, 'philosophy' means 'love of wisdom.' That's it. There are no veiled references to any particular philosophical system, even though many may think this subject has to do specifically and exclusively with ancient Greek thought that has become the foundation for western philosophy. Practically speaking, this guide helps us with gnosis; understanding gnosis, and applying it in our daily lives. This guide helps us understand the esoteric and subtle principles we encounter as we grow through life. As the occultist Dion Fortune said, to paraphrase, "while examples may change, the principles stay the same," meaning that even though the outer experiences we endure may change from generation to generation, the life lessons will basically stay the same. This is worth keeping in mind with this guide because they specialize in helping us understand the reasons behind things, so effectively, they help us understand human behavior and metaphysical underpinnings of the multiverse. Over the years I have gotten comfortable calling this guide my Doctor of Philosophy, but before I got to that point, I simply called him my "Mental Plane Guide." I share that here to let you know that minor changes like that can be applied to your guides, as long as it is in line with your spirituality and their traditional roles.

What is Gnosis?

The word 'gnosis' roughly means 'knowledge,' and this is the way it is commonly used today, but that is not the entire meaning. According to the dictionary, it means 'spiritual knowledge.' This has a dual meaning to it. First, yes, it means knowledge achieved through spiritual means and ways. Secondly, this could be interpreted as meaning accumulating knowledge about spiritual subjects. For example, many people achieve spiritual knowledge when they meditate on a moral, ethical, or spiritual quandary in their life. A good way to consider this is to think of those epiphanies you have had when you were engaging in practices like meditation or stillness. This means that yes, in a broad sense, everyone that has experienced this has achieved personal gnosis. If this information came about through guidance during a meditation or period of reflection, then they were probably guided by their Doctor of Philosophy guide.

As I wrote about in my book "*The Metaphysics of Magick*," there are two kinds of gnosis. There is "Verified Personal Gnosis (VPG)," and "Unverified Personal Gnosis (UPG)." The short description is that UPG is what you receive in meditation like we have been discussing, and it becomes VPG when it gets validated and verified by an outside source. Until then, it is highly subjective and open to debate. It may sound good, but other than being interesting material to consider, it really doesn't have any bearing or impact in a definitive sense. Personal gnosis becomes verified when we get a message from outside ourselves that aligns with it. Let us look at an example for clarification.

Let's say that you meditate on why it is wise to give wisdom that you receive, and the message you get is that the more you give, the more you receive. That by itself is unverified personal gnosis. It becomes verified personal gnosis when you hear this same teaching in your daily life, from someone that you have not told about this meditation insight. It becomes enforced or stronger personal gnosis when you hear that tidbit of wisdom from multiple people throughout your day. This simply reinforces the veracity of it. The Doctor of Philosophy guide will help you receive the gnosis, but whether it gets verified or not is another matter. Perhaps what you received in meditation was just meant to lift your spirits. Or perhaps what you received was meant to encourage you to think about a situation differently. Maybe the gnosis you received was not meant to be verified, but then again, maybe it was. There are a great many ways this can play out in daily life, so thinking that these situations *must* play out a certain way is an illogical pitfall to avoid.

Even though this is usually how the word gnosis is used today, there is another important point about it to discuss, which is that a few thousand years ago, Gnosticism, being gnostic, and gnosis, were all parts of a spiritual sect. There's not a lot to say about that here because I want to keep things focused on the Doctor of Philosophy, and not diverge into Gnosticism, but it does require a mention just in case you come across it on your own, or through the guidance of your Doctor of Philosophy guide. Many books have been written about the subject, and I see no reason to retread retrodden ground, but this point is worth mentioning because your guide may be leading you to that specific spiritual path. But it is also wise to know this because if you research this subject on your own, you may find your path is regularly guided back to Gnosticism specifically, when in reality, gnosis is a much greater, bigger, subject, not relegated to one specific movement thousands of years past.

Not What You Want to Hear…

Your Doctor of Philosophy Guide is approaching subjects, questions, etc. from the place of the mental plane, so approaches like logic, reason, detachment, and doing what is right, even if it feels uncomfortable, are all going to be common when you are in communication. For those that have issues with these subjects, you may find your relationship with this guide is rougher and more challenging than others. If you are too emotional, or too prone to escapism, this means that a relationship with this guide can be gut-wrenching and sometimes heartbreaking. As the title of this section implies, you may hear things from this guide that you do not want to hear, or like hearing, but they are important pieces of wisdom none the less.

All of this also means that it is wise to study logic, philosophy, and other mental and existential subjects to better facilitate dialogue with this good doctor. This does not have to be confined to Greek philosophy though. You can study modern psychology, or outdated Freudian psychology too, that can help you cultivate a better relationship with this guide. Or you can study the philosophies of eastern thinkers as well. Or both! 'Uncomfortable truths' is a good way to illustrate what it is like to work with this particular guide. Well, at least for this astrological water sign.

...But Exactly What You Need to Hear

I have found that the Doctor of Philosophy guide is an excellent balance when it comes to keeping control over your emotions and seeing things from varied points of view. Often, my philosophy guide has helped me process emotional situations that I was too mired in to see clearly. Conversely though, is the fact that my Doctor of Chemistry guide, who I will discuss soon, helps me offset my Doctor of Philosophy guide by bringing emotional awareness, heart intelligence, and intuitive development, all into balance and harmony with logic and reason. To some this may not seem like a good thing, but it really does help to see things as objectively as possible.

Here it should be pointed out though, that there are different parts of the mental plane, and because of that, we may hear what we need to hear from our Doctor of Philosophy guide, but it may not be communicated in a cold, logical way. Rather, messages may be conveyed through abstract thinking and thought. The mental plane is the plane of logic and reason, as discussed above, but the upper realms of the mental plane are abstract thinking. A good way to understand this is to think of mathematics. At the basic level, mathematics is black and white, with addition, subtraction, multiplication, and division, but when you get to the higher realms, such as algebra and trigonometry, it gets more abstract. This same concept is mirrored on the mental plane, so it is wise to be careful not to expect black and white interactions with this guide. Sometimes the interactions may include abstractions mixed with logic. Here I am reminded of a common school teaching in mathematics classes: "Solve for '*x*.'" Sometimes this is how your Doctor of Philosophy guide will communicate with us. It may give us part of the equation in order to guide us to the correct answer. Or it may overtly guide us in the initial steps of our thought process to understand something, but leave the middle and final parts of the equation for us to figure out. Really, this approach is a sign of wisdom, because effectively the guide is telling us where to look, but not what we will find, which is a hallmark of a good teacher.

For some people though, the Doctor of Philosophy does answer in black and white, and this is because of where one is at on their spiritual path. Perhaps this is a lifetime during which that is the best approach for the guide to reach us, and if this is the case, this is the route the guide will take to get through to us. If you are not a fan of logic, you may find that communicating with this guide results in black and white, cold, yes/no answers. If this should ever be the case with you, then ask yourself how you can go about seeing the world in a sliding scale of grey rather than a realm of absolutes. Most situations in life are somewhere in the grey matter, but oftentimes people fall into the trap of thinking situations are black and white. When I was much younger, this was the case with me. It was only through spiritual development and a lot of personal development work that I came to see the world on the grey scale.

It is because of all of these things that we can see our Doctor of Philosophy guide sometimes tells us what we need to hear, which could, in some instances, not be what we don't want to hear, but also what we should hear in order to grow. If you are wondering how your relationship with this guide will go, look at two major factors. The first is to look at your astrological chart. If your chart has a lot of the element of air in it, and all of it is harmonized well, then the relationship with your Doctor of Philosophy guide will be a good one, with a good mix of absolute and abstract approaches when it comes to helping you understand and learn things. This is also generally true if you have a lot of earth in your chart. But, if your chart is heavy with water and fire, you may find that your relationship with this guide is a little more fraught with challenges and potential miscommunications. It is oftentimes a challenge to blend your heart and your mind when it comes to decision making, so this can be a hurdle for many people. Working with ideas such as the heart intelligence and emotional intelligence can help, but there is a difference between knowing this and actually living it.

The second factor to look at is, bluntly, you! Are you more comfortable with logic than emotions, or emotions more so than logic? Are you highly creative but can't manage your finances? Does your heart constantly get you into trouble? What are your strengths? Are you surrounded by people that are more logical than emotional, or vice versa? And are you comfortable in their presence? If you have not started working with your guides yet, you can easily observe your life and circumstances to see what kind of interactions you will get with each guide. While I discuss this here, the concept applies to all of your guides, and we will put this under the microscope later in this book when we discuss specialty guides.

Once you look around at your life and assess your situation, then you can check to see if things are in or out of balance. Once this is determined, you know which guide to work with in order to bring things into better harmony. You may be a logical person surrounded by people that are emotional, as an example, and this can either be a good thing, as it brings emotional awareness to the forefront of your mind. Or, it can be a bad thing, because it limits how far you can develop your logic and mind in general. The way to determine which it is that is impacting you is to see the quality of your life, and the success you achieve. When the totality of the situation is assessed, you can then better cultivate your relationship with all of your guides.

Exercise Four: Follow the template ritual earlier in the book to contact your Doctor of Philosophy guide to further your work, but you can prepare for that by assessing your life, and seeing what you can expect from working with them. You may also find expanding your mind puts you in a better position to hear what the doctor has to say. Being well-rounded with various philosophies from various cultures is always a good thing, whether doing guide work or not, but in this case, it can be quite helpful when it comes to opening your mind to different approaches to handling life in general, which can make a large difference between success and failure. Almost every failure is a life lesson in and of itself though, which drives home the point that it is all in how you look at things, and how you formulate your responses. Advanced teachings having to do with the Doctor of Philosophy guide also cover the magical idea of consciously creating circumstances, so know that as much as I share here, there are more advanced techniques you may learn as you grow and develop, and many of those cannot and really should not, be discussed here. They are part of the inner mysteries, which many times cannot be conveyed at all.

Chapter Six: Your Doctor of Chemistry Guide

The Doctor of Chemistry guide is the one that is located to our left, and encompasses all things related to the emotional body, and to a lesser extent, the physical body of the individual. While its title is technically chemistry, this addresses more than just physical chemistry, as the title of this guide is a double entendre that addresses the chemistry that can happen between people as well. This concept uses the term chemistry in a very liberal way, but also addresses a lot of the metaphors of spirituality that we don't necessarily always catch. For example, the fact that we are 70-75% water, and water is an excellent conduit for energy, so thus humans are natural conduits for all of the energy of the multiverse. Another part of this concept is that we are all made of star matter, and this reminds us that strong potential lies within us at any given moment.

However, often our chemistry guide has their hands full because they address emotions, and the more emotionally invested someone is regarding a project or person, the more active this guide may end up being. It is true that we get a lot of energy from our emotions, and what is also true is that if we're not careful, our emotions can dictate our actions, for better or for worse, depending on the situation and our chosen response to it. Emotions are fuel, but out of control emotions can be destructive and toxic. Part of this correspondence also entails our intuition.

The Doctor of Chemistry guide is the primary guide when it comes to working with the emotions, but also the intuition. Thus, we discover that in order to work with our intuition, our Doctor of Chemistry guide can be the perfect assistant for us. Do you have a short temper? If so, then working with this guide can help with that. Do you put your heart on your sleeve too much, causing constant heartbreak? If so, this is the guide for you. Do you repress and suppress your emotions more than what is healthy? Yep, you guessed it - this is the guide that can help you fix that problem. This guide can also assist us when it comes to the affairs of the heart, and while this is covered under emotions, it is worth pulling out and addressing here because the heart is one of the most powerful seats of energy in the human energetic body.

What is Chemistry?

Let's break this down to deepen the discussion on the potency of this particular guide. The first meaning of chemistry is the one that we briefly discussed above. It is the ability of different substances to blend and get along with each, such as in the case of the chemistry between people, or the chemistry between a person and an organization. Reflect on times in your life when you immediately "meshed" with a certain person or when participating in a particular group. These would be examples of good chemistry. But then conversely, think of those times that you did not mesh well with either of those. Those are good examples of chemistry too, or more specifically, a lack of chemistry. Both meshing well and not meshing well fall under a broad definition of chemistry, personal chemistry, to be precise.

Then there is the actual subject of chemistry, a hard science that involves mixing various substances to produce a more potent and/or specific offspring. Chemistry, the science as it is today, is a development from the ancient subject of alchemy, the ability to turn lead into gold. If it wasn't for alchemy, chemistry would not exist. So yes, this means that your Doctor of Chemistry guide can help you learn actual chemistry, or alchemy, particularly spagyrics, which is plant-based alchemy. This means that you can work with this guide in a non-emotionally focused way. This can be useful when you are learning one of those subjects. I worked closely with my Doctor of Chemistry guide when I was learning alchemical fundamentals about fifteen years ago or so, to give you an example. On a fun note, this also means you could rename this guide your "alchemy guide," or "alchemical guide," if you do not like using the word "chemistry."

By extension then, you can see that this is the guide to work with if you are learning more modern forms of alchemy that use time-tested alchemical principles and processes to create spiritual gold from spiritual lead, or in changing the lead of the personality self into the gold of the spiritual self. This is another example of working with this guide to non-emotional ends. I feel knowing about all three of these non-emotionally focused subjects is key to understanding the potency and adaptability of the Doctor of Chemistry guide. It is not just a guide you work with when you are having emotional challenges. It is also a guide that can teach you esoteric principles through the study of these three subjects (chemistry, spagyrics, and spiritual alchemy), and their application in your life. Much more could be written about this point, but a lot of that would come from an in-depth discussion of alchemy, which is outside the scope of this book.

Emotional Intelligence

Over the last fifteen years or so there has been an increasing study of what is called heart intelligence, or emotional intelligence. This is a look at how emotions have an intelligence of their own, and when we develop our intuition, we are actually perfecting a decision-making process that is a blend between the heart and the mind, logic and emotions. While this may seem like some far-out or far-fetched notion, more and more scientific study is being done to show how this plays out in our physical bodies at a cellular level. This research is the result of investigating modern spiritual themes and thought tangents. Some may not agree with the science behind this, but the fact of the matter is that the more time that passes, the more data is collated and analyzed. When this happens for a long enough period of time, it will become established science, rather than something on the fringe, at least to conservative scientific minds. To more modern and liberal scientific minds, it is already seen as established science.

The principle of this is simple enough. The best way to proceed through life is to execute a decision-making process that is a blend of the heart and the mind. If you use nothing but your mind to make decisions, the lack of an intuition and emotions can be detrimental, and conversely, if you make decisions solely on your emotions, your life will suffer, too. This may seem radical to many people out there, but really it is the next step in the unfoldment of who and what we are as human beings. Every day science is discovering new information about our bodies and the world at large, and this should not be left out of our spiritual and personal growth. It is far too easy to learn your spiritual beliefs, and then rigidly get stuck, seemingly endlessly repeating habits and behavior based on outdated information. It happens to all of us if we're not careful. It has happened to me before, and it wasn't that I threw new information out, but rather I didn't learn or process new information as it came up. In some instances I outright rejected it, but that was because I didn't bother looking into it, or didn't reflect on its meaning and application. However, as time passed, these pieces of information kept coming up when I was researching various other topics, so eventually I could not turn a blind eye. I researched them, internalized them, applied them, and in the process, found that my spiritual path was enhanced because I opened my mind. When that happened enough times, I learned

(Sometimes I am hard-headed!) to research these topics as they came up and to keep an open mind as to how they can enhance my spiritual and personal growth.

As one achieves a successful integration and application of the heart-centered intelligence, they usually find this impacts their health in positive ways. If you want to know more about that, I would consider consulting a qualified professional, and while I can point you in this direction, you will have to do that work on your own. The impetus for doing this work on your own though, rather than relying on me to tell you, is that recent DNA discoveries have found that trauma is passed down through DNA to the next generation. For example, if your mother or father experienced a particular life-altering trauma when they were younger, you, the child, will receive that trauma. So, if your parent had a near fatal drowning incident and never swam again, then you could possibly be aquaphobic, or have an irrational fear of drowning. Other than justifying the necessity of emotional health and healing, this also helps explain concepts like generational karma, superstitious family curses, etc. Up until now those ideas were considered subject to personal subjective beliefs, but more and more data is revealing this is scientifically true. In some ways this corroborates the age-old idea of the sins of the father being passed down to the son, and in some ways, this corroborates the idea of original sin, but both of those are subjects to discuss for another time and place.

For now it is enough to know that when you decide to work with your Doctor of Chemistry guide, you can achieve a lot of healing and growth, not just for yourself, but also future generations that you may produce. Even if you do not plan on reproducing, this is still something worth considering, because it can help you understand the people that produced you, and in turn, this can help save some future incarnations by dealing with things now that have been held over from several previous lifetimes. Just like our DNA carries ingrained patterns on a physical level, our soul retains ingrained patterns, too, and by working with one, you work with the other as well.

More than Romantic Love

A lot of people think that the best reason to work with your Doctor of Chemistry guide is to achieve success in affairs of the heart, but there is so much more than that, that can be accomplished. First as hinted at above, there is the topic of emotional healing. Working with this guide can help you heal those emotionally traumatic wounds that are present in your heart and psyche. I don't really think I need to explain this point much more than this. This affects all emotions, so the person that has anger management issues could execute healing as much as the widow healing a broken heart. The narcissist can heal as much as those with low self-confidence. All of this also infers that the more someone is compassionate, forgiving, emotionally available, and understanding, the more you can see that they are in touch with this guide.

Next we have the development of the intuition. In addition to romantic goals, this is probably the second most popular reason people have for working with their Doctor of Chemistry guide. This is a popular subject in modern spiritual circles because a common teaching is to listen to your intuition. Another way to look at it is "follow your heart but lead with your head." Yes, your heart and intuition may tell you to go one direction, but that does not mean you have to resign yourself to that path with reckless abandon. In your pursuit of following your intuition, it is wise to keep your wits about you. Another common modern spirituality teaching is that the body is the subconscious mind, so when you are listening to your intuition, you are effectively listening to what your body is telling you, as it is interpreted and filtered through your subconscious. This is another teaching that started off as an esoteric secret and teaching but has now come under greater scientific scrutiny over the last twenty years or so. I have found this to be true on average, but if you have had a different experience, then so be it. I have not done any deep research into the subject, so I could not tell you if my perception is in the minority or majority of experiences, so here is the map, but you will have to learn the territory.

Third, just to reiterate, is that you can learn chemistry and alchemy with the assistance of your Doctor of Chemistry guide. And you can choose which kind of alchemy to learn - spagyrics or spiritual. It is quite the paradox to consider the fact that you could learn a scientific subject like chemistry through working with this guide. Superficially it may seem like that should be aligned with the Doctor of Philosophy guide, but that is not the case for one big reason above all others. Both chemistry and alchemy rely heavily on experimentation using physical resources, and there is quite the esoteric lesson here that is being revealed. The lesson is that your life is the petri dish to use for experimentation when it comes to spirituality and occultism. Part of this lesson is also that you achieve more spiritual success if you take on the mentality of a spiritual scientist. This is something that has only been discussed for about the last one hundred years or so. Before that, success in magick and spiritual development was believed to be based on religiosity and spiritual purity, and we have learned over the last one hundred years, that that is not necessarily the case. Yes, purity in those two areas can help and does matter, but it is not the be-all-end-all for success.

Following this tangent of thought, it is also worth noting that this is the guide to work with if you want to improve your astral projection ability, or to trigger an out-of-body experience. I realize many people might never go this far or in this direction when it comes to developing their relationship with the Doctor of Chemistry guide, but to me, this is an important point to know. Water is the conduit that flows between the planes, and when you begin to mix various substances as is commonly the case of alchemy, you create effects that can trigger out-of-body experiences and perceptions. Technically, yes, you can also get out of your body with the help of your Doctor of Philosophy guide, but that is a trip (!) to the mental plane, which is higher, more abstract, and different to the astral plane. One of the ways you can work with this information is to astral travel with your Doctor of Chemistry as your guide through those finer planes. Many people do not use a guide when they leave their body, but you can do this if you so choose. I have done it before once or twice, and I did that when I was just learning the skill. Since I have refined it, I no longer work with a guide, but I can speak from personal experience when I say that it is a viable route to take to get where you want to go.

Power!

In occultism and modern spirituality, it is often times said that emotions give us the fuel and the power necessary to accomplish our goals and achieve our desires. When you put things together, you see that the gatekeeper is our protector, the philosophical doctor helps us plan, understand, and give form to our thoughts, and our chemical doctor helps us develop and focus the necessary energy to get things done. All of this is done under the guidance and oversight of our master teacher. When you look at their roles in this way, you can see how everything fits together. For those of you that are familiar with Qabalism and the western esoteric tradition, you will see that this also lines up with the YHVH formula and the four worlds of the qabala. I won't go into details here, but I do feel this is an important point to know so that we see how everything connects together.

The more emotionally invested one is in their life and their projects, the more success they can achieve, and the more they can learn. This is the biggest reason to work with your emotions, and to develop a relationship with your Doctor of Chemistry. Learning how to harness the power of your emotions can go a long way to manifesting your desired results, and therefore your desired life. Controlling and guiding emotions does not mean suppressing them. They mean putting emotions to work for you, rather than being strung along by your emotions. And let's face it, if you are strung along by your emotions, then you are probably constantly reacting to situations instead of being proactive co-creating your reality.

Keep in mind that on the other side of the veil, many beings see emotions as food, so the more emotional control you have, the more you are protecting yourself. Untrained and unrestrained emotions can be used against you in a multitude of ways. These ways do not have to be psychological, either. The idea of "mob rule" and all of the toxicity that implies comes to mind here, as an example of how this can manifest in the physical world. Your emotions can cloud your judgment, as well as get you to think and process things in a vastly different way than what is healthy. Sometimes heightened emotions can be good, such as the adrenaline created by a panicked parent that lifts a car to save their child, but more often than not, people have their emotions manipulated much to their detriment and disempowerment.

As you can tell from the heading of this section, working with this guide can greatly increase your personal power, which you can then funnel into your physical world projects and goals. While the Doctor of Philosophy guide is all about understanding, the Doctor of Chemistry guide is about healing and tapping into your personal power. This is also the guide to work with for more esoteric reasons, like the astral projection mentioned above. While all of these are good points to work with, they are also warnings. If you work with this guide too much, emotional problems may be the least of yours. Pride, toxic ego, and other psychological maladies may come about from excessing emotional body work.

Well then, what is personal power? There are many different definitions of this phrase, so it would be outside the scope of this book to do a deep dive on the subject, but I do want to touch on a few key things to illustrate how your Doctor of Chemistry guide can help you. Having and using personal power is of utmost importance to those that are serious about their growth, and in a lot of ways, it is available to everyone. Not everyone has the same level of personal power though, and this should be kept in mind. What one person is good at may not be a strength to another person.

According to psychologytoday.com, "personal power is based on strength, confidence, and competence that individuals gradually acquire in the course of their development. It is self-assertion, and a natural, healthy striving for love, satisfaction, and meaning in one's interpersonal world."

Personally, I like this definition, as it is exacting but open enough to be analyzed further. You can see how this is a process, and one that repeats itself through life in various circumstances as we grow and develop. Personal power is also not an absolute, as you may have a lot of personal power in one area of your life, but in another area, it is lacking. Regardless of the finer points in this paragraph and the ideas that stem from pondering them, the Doctor of Chemistry guide can help us develop our own. At this point it would be wise to take a few moments and reflect on your personal power - where it is at in some areas of your life, and where it could be improved on in other areas. When you complete this brief exercise, you have a good starting point to work with your Doctor of Chemistry. Often the key to working through and healing your personal power is through emotional investment in the process and also to face the emotional wounds that are the source of the lack of personal power. We should be mindful though, that the development of personal power is an ongoing process. This means one cannot rest on their laurels once they accomplish their desired personal growth. To temper this though, remember that the constant pursuit of power is toxic and destructive, so moderation should be practiced. Be careful not to give up your personal power, but also remember that compromise is the key to working with others for success in life.

You can now see a lot of the range that the Doctor of Chemistry guide has, and circling back to the beginning of the chapter, it is clear that this guide is not only about romantic love, or even just 'love.' Your relationship with this guide can be quite profound and life-changing, but it can also be wrought with facing and healing emotional wounds. This can also be the second strongest guide to work with for spiritual growth right after the Master Teacher guide. When working with this guide, it would be wise to avoid underestimating what this guide can do. This can be a bitter pill to swallow for those that have emotional issues and unresolved wounds and lack the courage to face them.

Exercise Five: Using the popular Spirit Guide Contact Template from chapter two, make contact with your Doctor of Chemistry Guide, and record your findings in your journal. Pay special attention to how you feel while working with this guide.

Chapter Seven: Your Secondary Spirit Guides

Unlike the primary spirit guides we all have from birth that we just finished discussing, there are other spirit guides that may only be with us for a short time. There are also guides we all have that don't fit into the schema of the primary guides, and we will address those as well. We somewhat enter into uncharted territory here because Spiritualism hasn't done a lot to codify or structure this area, so in a lot of ways we are on our own. This is great for subjective interpretation and for making all of this work together on an individual level in one's personal paradigm. Because of this, we have a shorter yet broader list to discuss.

The same spiritual and universal laws apply here, in that these beings have energetic connections to us, most of which were established by contracts before birth. The nature of these relationships vary from person to person, but have to do with each particular guide. Not all of these guides are with us for life. Yes, some of them can be with us for life, but many don't stay with us that long. The relationships with these guides change over the course of life, and this is especially true of animal guides. Some of these guides are not external beings, while some are.

When it comes to contacting and working with them, the same approaches and techniques that are used with primary guides can also be used here. The gist of it is to remember that they are spirits, so any techniques you know or are comfortable with can be used here. They support us like the other guides do, but the nature of their relationships will vary from time to time. Some of them may be with us for a long period of time, while others may only be around for a few months. It is nearly impossible to give details here, as I am in physical form and therefore limited to the knowledge available, so keep that in mind while working through this material.

All of this also tells us you have a large amount of control over which of these guides you choose to work with, rather than knowing there are four mainstays, as in the case of the other guides. Stories of people working with spirits go back centuries, which tells us it is not uncommon to work with spirits for a variety of reasons. Occultism has addressed this in depth over the centuries by discussing the skills of invocation and evocation, but this is a different relationship and style of spirit interaction. What we're talking about here is a different type of relationship. These relationships involve karmic connections a lot more than invocation or evocation does. Additionally, these are gentler relationships. Like your primary guides, these are supportive beings that have a strong, positive, energetic connection with you and a sincere desire to help you evolve.

Let's look at several different types of guides we will have through life in addition to the main four. We will look at their characteristics and will discuss what to expect from these relationships. We will also discuss ways through which we can be proactive when it comes to our futures while we are in physical form. In a lot of ways, we are more empowered in these relationships than we are regarding others because these are more fluid. This also means the nature of these relationships is more relaxed and cooperative, they are more adaptable to your spiritual paradigm. And, best of all, there is even less dogma involved here than in the context of the four primary guides. Those are structured via Spiritualism, but these are more of a collection of spirit guides from various places looked at through various lenses. Some of these may be familiar, while others may seem alien, but I assure you, that no matter how you view them this may inspire spiritual growth in unexpected directions.

Specialty Guides

This is a broad category of guides and in this way is a catch-all for whatever guide doesn't fit in any other category. The one underlying theme they all have is that they are specialists first and foremost, they are not general purpose. This means that if you have a financial guide, do not expect it to be good handling affairs of the heart, it will help you with finances of many types, yes, and it will do well in that regard, but that will be the extent of its role and assistance. Many times people will pick up specialty guides incidentally. For example, if you lose your job and get a new one that you may not be as competent with, you may be so focused on learning that you unknowingly pick up a specialist guide of that type. If you reverse engineer this thought though, you can also see that if you are wanting to change careers or take yours to the next level, you can intentionally cultivate a relationship with a specialty guide of that type.

We can then infer that our karmic relationships to these guides are not as strong or developed as our main four guides, and while that is generally true, it is also not completely accurate. Your soul may want to take this lifetime to perfect the art of accounting, for example, and in order to do this, you come into this life with an accounting guide as a specialty guide. After this life is resolved, your soul and the guide would then discuss where to grow from there, based on how the lifetime played out. Existentially, you can see that it is entirely possible for a specialty guide to transition to one of your four main ones, given other factors._It can be deduced that on average, these guides will be around for the shortest period of time due to the nature of our relationships with them.

This is something I have worked with many times in my life, as circumstances have routinely come up that have caused me to have to make many changes in employment and professional direction. The way I have worked with this is to pull in specialty guides to either A) guide me towards a particular profession, or B) assist me in taking my then current professional trajectory to the next level. This has been both successful and not, and varied by circumstances. Most times it has been successful, but in unexpected ways. Often what I have found is that the specialty guide or guides in question will do just that - guide. They have led me to job openings, or people I need to know to professionally develop, but whether I pass the interview or make a good enough impression on who I meet, is all up to me. Sometimes the way this has played out is that the specialty guide led me to pertinent research that showed me that the career I was thinking of taking was not a good fit for me at all. Or the guide led me to see that a career I had passed over may be better than I thought it could be. Regardless of the end result, I can say for certain that by keeping your mind open, you will see the value of what your specialty guide or guides brings to the table.

Yes, you can have more than one specialty guide at a time. This was true for me quite often when I was younger and carving out a career for myself. I had a specialty guide that would help me with my day job, and a specialty guide that would help me professionally develop in this direction. The biggest challenge I had in these cases was to not get too dependent or reliable on those particular guides. At first it was far too seductive to "let go and let guide," to corrupt a phrase. As you probably see, this led me to laziness and a lack of ambition. I had to step up my work ethic in order to seize and maximize the opportunities my specialty guides provided. Part of those life lessons had to do with personal responsibility and personal accountability, but some of them had to do with learning the limits of what specialty guides can and can't do. Due to the subjective nature of all of this, it took me a lot of time to work with and apply these thoughts, but in time, I did, much to my benefit. Unfortunately, while that was occurring I was having little to no luck finding information in books about all of this because, bluntly, these finer points are not discussed, so I had to proceed slowly and cautiously in order to be thorough and as objective as possible so that I could share this with others. This tempo was compounded by the fact I was working with more than one specialty guide, which slowed everything down. In time though, I did achieve success with my specialty guides.

It is wise to not become too reliant on them, though, which leads us to the next point. When working with them, be very clear in your mind what information comes from them, and what information is yours. Working with spirit guides is supposed to be an enhancement to life, not a substitute for hard work. Besides personal responsibility, personal accountability, and a strong work ethic, other character traits you can develop are dedication, discipline, and accountability, so you can see there are many benefits to doing things yourself. Guides will lead us where we should go, but it is up to us to take advantage of the desired situations, even if they are not what we thought they would be. Let's use an example to illustrate that point. Let's say you are considering becoming a veterinarian, but you have no experience. You call in a specialty guide to help you with this, and it leads you to an in-depth article by someone in the industry that precisely outlines all of the necessary steps it takes to be a professional veterinarian. You read the article and realize that while you like the idea of helping animals, the personal investment is too much for where you're at in life. Some may think that this is the end of the story, but there is still another piece to it. Now that you know that particular path is not for you, you can still be in that environment in a number of ways. You could get a job as a receptionist at a veterinarian's office, or you could go into work as a driver that makes deliveries of necessary supplies. I give these two examples here, but there is no limit to the creative imagination. Both of these examples would put you in close proximity with veterinarians. Both would achieve your goal of helping animals. Even if you look into these directions and still find it is not for you, you can still hold your head high and feel confident about giving the situation your all. The only thing left to do at this point is to thank your specialty guide, end the relationship, and move on to the next possibility.

The Importance of Gratitude

Did that surprise you? Did you think about showing gratitude when you see how your specialty guides helped you? Yes, gratitude is important when working with spirit guides, but how you show it is largely up to you. Usually, the way I see it is simply to give prayers of thanks, but I have known people in the past that did something fancier, like setting up a gratitude altar in their home, or making offerings if they know what their guides would want. Showing gratitude to various spirits for various reasons is one of the most important things to do not just in this case, but also in general. The more you express your thankfulness, the more you invite those spirits, and others, to work with you in the future. Working with spirits is a lot like working with flesh-and-blood people. Both like to know that they are appreciated. Both should be treated with respect. Many other parallels exist, but I highlight these two to show why gratitude is important. Sometimes you may not know what the spirit wants as a gift of gratitude, and that is okay. That is also why I like to offer prayers and thanks. I work with a lot of different spirits, and I believe in working smarter, not harder. If you work with a small number of spirits, then you are in a better position than I to know the preferences of the spirits, and if this is the case, then I encourage you to do so. Regardless of how you handle this, consider this point before starting serious, long-term guide work.

Old Friends

Yes, sometimes your specialty guides may have been people you knew in past lives. I have not found this to be the norm, but I have also not found this to be exceedingly rare, either. Usually the situation goes something like this: you (the understood you, and not you, specifically, reading this.) find you have a certain knack for a job or a skill. You begin to spiritually and personally develop, and you find that you have a specialty guide that helps you professionally advance. Then, after much meditation and skill development, you find out that you knew this guide in another life, and in that life, you helped them out in some personal area of their life. This life, then, is them returning the favor by helping you with something that they know a lot about. Most times this information cannot be verified, so it would stay UPG, but in some cases you can find specific information if desired. If that occurs, then the information can change and become VPG. It is wise to not seek to verify this information, as that can actually make things harder for you. Rather, it is wiser to just let the situation unfold organically.

With a little thinking, you can also see that your relationships today may lead to guide relationships with others in future lives. If you are a mentor to someone in the professional world, and they are succeeding with what you teach them, then the potential is there for you to be a specialty guide for them in a life when they are in physical form and you are not. While I use the professional world as an example here, this idea is not confined to just professions and careers. Really, this can happen in almost every area of life. The interesting part of this is that if you and the other person in the example are in physical form, then you can discuss these topics while both of you are alive. This conversation should not be undertaken lightly, but it can be taken nonetheless. This opens the mind to the many ways that finer energies can be manipulated in the multiverse. While this may seem like a radical idea, it is an ages-old idea in some eastern traditions, especially those that involve sorcery.

Tibetan sorcery comes to mind here, and the various ways energy is manipulated during one's life, across the veil, and extending over lifetimes. I only hint at this here, because books have been written about this subject, and there is no way I can do it justice here. I simply offer it as an example of a group of people that have taken this idea to an extreme, and if I am aware of one and mention it here, then there are probably many other organizations that I do not know about that have done such things, if not more. I also encourage extensive, documented, experimentation on this point. After all, what an amazing idea to consider! Creating a whole mystery school that incorporates this to an extreme degree is a fascinating subject to ponder, isn't it?

I have news for you. Such groups do exist already, and when we study occultism and metaphysics, we find that idea extended almost infinitely on the printed page. The White Lodge from theosophy comes to mind here, as does the (argued) Secret Chiefs of the Hermetic Order of the Golden Dawn. There are many more that are part of this conversation, but for the sake of brevity I will curtail things here. I simply take us down this to stimulate your imagination when it comes to working with these concepts and ideas in your spiritual paradigm. After all, what a wonderful show of friendship it is to reincarnate together, or to have arranged relationships like these. Let your imagination flow, and if you feel so inclined, develop them internally or with others you know.

Logistics

Earlier we established where in the circle of your aura your four primary guides are located (in front of you, behind you, to your right, and to your left), so let us take a brief moment to discuss the placement of specialty and secondary guides. Technically, they are not located at any particular spot in your circle. On one hand, this tells us that they can be wherever they show you they are, and on the other hand, this tells us they may move around as you work with them. For many years, my joy guide showed herself as a woodland sprite, and would constantly be moving around me when I worked with her in a very impish, pixie way. Thus, test for yourself where various specialty and secondary guides are. In the beginning of your development, you may find a pendulum is the most appropriate tool for the job, but as you progress and develop, you may move away from needing any tools at all.

Many times, people share secondary or specialty guides, and really, this makes sense. A friend of mine was a professional nurse for 40+ years. She was many things, but she was a Spiritualist, too, and she had a specialty nurse guide. Her thought was that since she only worked with her nurse guide when she was doing nursing duties, it made no sense that the guide would be around her when she was not. Remember that sharing is caring, meaning that the more things are shared for the betterment of all, the better quality of life is created for all. I agree with her on this point. It does not make sense that the specialty guide would stay around when you are not working with them. And, since there is not time or space on the other side of the veil, then it stands to reason that they could be working with someone else that is in physical form in their area of expertise, when they are needed there. In that we, we may share guides with others. This also means that if you are not actively working with them, they may not appear to you in meditation, or it may be harder to make contact with them. In these instances, that is not a bad thing, even though we may question our power and ability.

We will now discuss some of the more common specialty and secondary guides, but this list and conversation is by no means exhaustive. Simply take this list and add or subtract to it as you see fit, but this can simply define a starting point for your further studies.

Exercise Six: When you finish reading the following material, it is time for the next exercise, which is simply listing your secondary and specialty guides. Compile a list of their names, appearances, and identifying symbols. Feel free to add other traits, too, or even to remove some of the ones listed here.

Joy Guide

One of the more popular and documented spirit guides, the joy guide is a common one that people encounter early in their development. Everything we need to know about this guide can be found in its name. This guide helps us laugh and find joy in everyday life. This means that sometimes it makes us laugh at ourselves, which can be quite the humbling experience. It is generally considered to be one of the oldest guides that we have. In this context, oldest means age, rather than how long it has been with us. Joy guides are often considered to be very advanced, wise souls. They teach us wisdom through humor, which sometimes includes dark humor, depending on who we are. In a lot of ways, they remind me of the archetype of the jester, or The Fool card from the tarot. When working with this guide, remember though that the sense of humor will be that of the guide's perspective, and not necessarily yours. If you remember this when working with them, you will most likely find yourself humbled, but possessing of profound wisdom over the course of development of your relationship with it. Something that is funny to the joy guide may not be funny to us, at least initially. Many times my joy guide has done something funny that I did not agree with, and while at the time I did not find it funny, after time had passed, I did find it funny. Even though I did not agree with it, I at least understood where the spirit was coming from, and in the process, I learned about the guide and spirits in general.

Inner Child Guide

Technically, this is not a guide in the true sense like we have been discussing here, but I include it in this text due to the similarities between the relationship between you and your inner child, and the relationship you have with your other guides. This is the representation of who you are on the inside. We're not talking the mature, adult you, though, we're talking about that part of you that is young, innocent, child-like, creative, playful, and whimsical. Many people lose touch with this part of them as they grow into adulthood and have various life experiences, so it is fairly routine to meet someone that thinks they do not have an inner child, or worse, that their inner child is malicious. Everyone has childlike qualities in them, but not everyone has a healthy relationship with that part of themselves. Being out of internal balance in this area can manifest as many health problems, and the irony of the situation is that one of the most effective healing modalities to remedy this is to become more childlike.

More and more research is being done into the connection between joy, happiness, and good health, which gives us even more motivation to cultivate this connection. How do you connect with your inner child? What playful, innocent things do you do, that allow you to let that part of you out? For some people, it is playing in a bouncy house. For others it is playing a musical instrument. Still others find their youthfulness restored by playing sports or engaging in artistic development. For me its indulging in games of various types. What is it for you? If you do not have this in your life, then I would strongly encourage you to develop something. Even if what you develop seems small, the fact that you take that initial step is what matters. You can add to it and change it later as you grow and develop.

Many times our inner child gets repressed not only as we grow through life, but also due to trauma suffered in childhood. Because of this, when we start to work with our inner child, we drudge up childhood traumas and wounds so that we can heal them and grow. As you have probably already guessed, this is easier said than done, but I mention it here for those of you that may encounter these instances. This also means that before you start working with your inner child, it is wise to have your life in order enough so that if unexpected trauma comes up, you can deal with it, without losing control of your entire life.

Since the inner child is part of our psyche, the line blurs between objective and subjective reality. You could say that when you work with your inner child, you are *just* working with your mind, but then again, in occultism and modern spirituality, working with your mind in many ways is par for the course, as the saying goes. Even if you just develop your psychic senses, you are still *just* working with your mind. This detailed point has been discussed extensively in various places over the last one hundred years or so, and even though this perspective has its critics, I have yet to see it deconstructed. The line between objectivity and subjectivity is blurred, and getting more blurred every day, due to scientific discoveries and a growing body of data. Recent science has demonstrated that most of what we call reality is subjective for the most part, rather than objective. With this being the case, we can say that it is irrelevant whether the inner child is a part of our psyche or a separate spirit altogether. The fact of the matter is that this is present, it exists, and it is now up to us to do the work.

Chapter Eight: Your Ancestor Guides

By now it should be clear that most or all of these topics are extensively covered in other books and media, so for those of you that want to know more about a particular topic, you will find a plethora of material with a minimal search. This is especially true when we turn our attention to ancestor guides. Working with ancestor guides, and ancestor worship in general, is one of the oldest spiritual traditions on the planet, dating back thousands of years. Because death is the only constant, this has even been studied across various disciplines, ranging from academia to religion and beyond. It is due to this that I will be brief with my remarks here. There are several types of ancestors one works with through life, and this chapter will give you a rough overview of several of them.

When I first learned about ancestor work, I took a natural liking to it. I completely understand why it is common, and has been for a long, long time. Most people learn about ancestors and death early in life, so it logically follows that contemplating death and those that have come before us is a natural development in our formative years. At least that is what I thought, then. Times have changed though, and I have learned and changed a lot since that time. Part of that change has been in learning that not everyone has a natural curiosity about death, and then by extension, about those that have come before. Now, many decades older and wiser (?), I have learned that a great number of people do not have any interest in either of these topics: death and ancestors. I should have figured this out many years ago, but *que serra serra*.

For many people, the immediate family and formative years is a sore subject. Generally, this is because of trauma suffered in childhood at the hands of said immediate loved ones. Some, though, are not interested in this because they were adopted or abandoned by their parents. I understand both of those points, and I can understand why someone would not want to work with these guides, so if you are one of those people, then feel free to skip this section. After all, these are really secondary guides, so as with almost anything in life, the choice is up to you whether or not you work with and incorporate this material. Be warned though, that I will be writing this chapter from the perspective of trying to convince everyone to work with these particular guides and practices, so I do have an agenda. It may not be the agenda you think, though, so if you read further into this chapter, be forewarned.

DNA

Like the inner child, these are different kinds of guides, because they are connected to us through blood and DNA. Earlier we discussed the power of genetic memories, and that general concept comes into play here as well. Regardless of your relationship with your birth family, and regardless of the traumas you experienced as a child, you have DNA. This DNA came from a set of DNA (Mother and Father/Sperm and Egg), and is a product, but not a replica, of them. If you know your parents, then you have kind of figured out what to expect when it comes to habits and patterns inherited from them. For example, if your mother had a short temper, then it stands to reason that you do, too. Or, if your father was prone to addictions, then genetically you have a predisposition to them, as well. These ideas are part of the touchy subject of ancestor guides, and really, just ancestors in general. It takes courage to acknowledge this and honestly face it. Depending on your circumstances and experiences, this might also be an ongoing, lifelong process of discovery.

If you know who your parents are, and have spent at least minimal time around them, then you know what to expect, in a rough and general sense. It is relatively easy to pick up on behavior patterns of our parents if we are indeed around them. Sometimes this information takes the form of family legends and stories too. The more that we grow, the more we learn about them as adults rather than as parents, and this means that more character traits become obvious to us. Life happens, and because of this, we can learn about our parents and grandparents when they react to situations. We can also learn about them by knowing what circumstances they had to face during the course of their lives. People that lived through the Great Depression developed the trait of hoarding, as an example, and making do with what was present and available. This meant developing humility but could also mean developing feelings of unworthiness. You can see how this becomes a complex subject with little to no effort or though.

If you do not know who your parents are, it does make things a little trickier. In this case, you have to self-evaluate in order to reverse engineer this information. If you know you have a short temper, then you can assume it runs in the family. Or, if you are prone to addictions, you can assume it is carried in the DNA in your bones as well. If you get stumped, you can always ask friends what they think of your character, specifically focusing on character traits like these. Yes, these are assumptions, so take them with a grain of salt. As I have discussed previously, I am a firm believer that we choose our parents before birth, so we choose to have certain experiences, even though we may not know why while we are alive.

Regardless of the particulars, you can easily understand the gist of who you are, and that puts you in a position to figure out your DNA traits. If you do not know who your parents are, you are in an advantageous position simply due to the fact that you are starting this lifetime with a clean slate. You are really more empowered simply because you do not have any preconceived notions to address. The most prominent situation you have to address is whatever bio-physiological health situations occur. For example, if you do not know who your parents are but the doctor tells you that you have a heart murmur, then you know some of your family karma to address has to do with not only physical heart health, but also emotions and the astral plane.

If you do know who your parents are, then you learn other traits, such as personality, etc. This means that yes, you can learn more about why you are here if you know who your parents are, and the traits and situations they have had to deal with, but it also means that you also see the parameters you have to work within when it comes to your personal growth. No one likes to hear that they have limits, but this is a fact none the less.

Spiritual Ancestor Guides

Now that we have discussed genetic ancestors, let's turn our attention to the other end of the spectrum, which are our spiritual ancestors. This is a chosen group of guides that all share the common thread of your spiritual traditions and practices. Okay, well, that is not entirely true. Sometimes these guides are not chosen, but rather attached to us through DNA memory like we discussed earlier. For example, if you are from a Roman Catholic family, but are not Roman Catholic, you may find that a lot of your ancestors were Catholic, and in that way, Catholicism is tied to your DNA, so you may have to encounter and deal with Catholic lessons and dogma throughout your life. These guides are only partially tied to us genetically like the other guides are, but they have taken a liking to us in this life, or we arranged this with them before we came into physical form. In any case, these are spirits that we work with when we are engaging in our spiritual practices. Some people work with deities of various pantheons in these roles, but others do not. It is entirely up to you but understand, that if it is a god or a goddess, it is not the *totality* of the deity.

This is something that is not discussed a lot in the Western Esoteric Tradition, but is quite common in eastern traditions, especially Hinduism. This is the idea of the avatar. In short, an avatar is basically a shard of the soul of the overall deity. The working theory behind this is that the deity or spirit does not need to send all of its power and potency to help you. It can send just a shard or a sliver. In Hinduism, the avatars of various deities have developed stories around them, and are quite deep and colorful, with profound morals and lessons. For our purposes, it is not necessary to go in-depth about that here. Simply knowing about this soul-shard/avatar idea is enough. This also explains how many people can receive blessings from the same deity at the same time across the globe. This is also how many people can be in touch with the goddess Isis at the same time, either in a ritual or informal setting. To understand this, remember just how massive the consciousness of a deity truly is. And the older and more followed the deity the more potent the power. This also means that as spirits are forgotten, their power diminishes. This point is more of a detail than anything else, but it is important to be aware of, in case you meet someone that has the same spiritual guide as you do. This is a logical, metaphysical explanation of how this can occur. People that do not know this point many times get miffed if someone else has the same guide as them in this context. I've seen some people get jealous over this, and some even claim that the other person's guide is a fraud! Yes, people can get petty over this fairly quickly, so I share this so that you do not become one of those people.

If you have a spiritual ancestral guide that you are working with, do not feel like it has to be a particular deity. Some of my spiritual guides are not deities from my spiritual traditions, but rather are beings that lived there during the times that I work with the most. If I work with a deity, it is not in the capacity of a spirit guide or associate that we are discussing here, and the reason for that is that I do my best to stay humble and know my place. For example, if I need protection, I generally don't call on one of the more popular protective beings because they are busy with other, more serious situations. Not everyone shares that view, but I mention it here to illustrate an approach you can take.

Besides, remember what we discussed earlier, that spirits may give us a false name, and that can be changed later, but also that is not necessarily a bad thing. You never know if the random spirit you are working with as a spirit guide is actually a more potent spirit. The easy way to handle this as I have learned is to simply treat every spirit with respect. That way, you cannot be surprised if a name switch occurs. And, just to emphasize, this sort of name switch does not happen often. It is just something to be mindful of as you spiritually grow and develop.

At this point it is also wise to keep in mind that if you are working with an "average Joe" spirit from a particular spiritual tradition, and it is not a name from a particular more powerful spirit, then that spirit is one that has not gone beyond to its next incarnation or higher vibrational state of being. In short, they would be considered earth bound, even though they're technically not. Really, they are "you" bound, for various energetic and karmic reasons. We can theorize and hypothesize all we want as to why the link is there, but the fact of the matter is that we really won't know until we leave physical form behind at the end of our life. They are limited to the experiences, technology, and society where they last lived. It has been my experience this is another detail to simply note, and in the long run, of minor consequence. If you look at the evolution of humanity, you can easily see that people generally don't change, or change very slowly. Character traits like greed, lust, jealousy, and pride have all been around since the dawn of time, and they show no signs of going away anytime soon. So, their strength is not just in their knowledge and application of the spiritual tradition you connect with, but also in knowing human nature. I have learned a lot about human nature from the help of my spiritual guides, because they can see subtle energetic patterns that we may not. They also have particular insights that we are not privy to, so it is always wise to pursue every line of thought that comes up when dealing with them.

Besides all of these points, spiritual ancestor guides can also help us understand cultural and social karma. Often a soul is reincarnated into a particular society or culture to work through life lessons associated with them. If a spiritual guide of yours is not from your culture, then they can help you understand whatever culture birthed them. When I visited Egypt a number of years ago, I did a lot of work with a guide of mine that was from that spiritual tradition, and it led me to have a deeper understanding of that culture. That extended to the society of that land as well, and in this way, I learned practical, applicable information, perspectives, and ways to handle situations that come up in my daily life. Much like human nature, society really has not evolved that much over the last several thousand years. Social traits like human trafficking, religion, sex work, artistic expression, and commerce have all been around since Mesopotamia, which is considered the foundation of the modern city from city planner and architectural perspectives.

***

The Chosen Few

So far we have discussed genetic and spiritual guides, but there are several other types of ancestral guides you may pick up through life. This is to be expected, since all of us are at different points on our spiritual path, but I mention them here for the sake of completeness. There is not a lot I can address though, because this is so subjective, but I will share some preliminary thoughts that may be of use as you cultivate your relationships with your spirit associates.

Because this is uncharted waters in a lot of ways, there is not a lot I can say, but I will hit some key points to consider. First, note when a new spiritual guide makes their presence known to you. They may be arriving because of something that is coming up in your life, rather than as the result of work you've already done. They might be telling you that something from their spiritual tradition may be of help in life situations on the horizon. Or they could be leading you in the next direction of your growth on your path. Because of this, it would be wise to always keep an open mind when recognizing them and interpreting why they are in your life. Being dismissive of them would not be wise.

Secondly, and I cannot stress this enough, be open minded! Sometimes a guide from a spiritual tradition from your past may show up. There may be a tendency to carte blanche ignore it, especially if you have unhealed wounds from that tradition, but that would be unwise to do. The reason for this is that they do have some sort of message for you, even if it makes you uncomfortable. The ability to listen to what the guide has to say is a skill developed by the wise, regardless of where it originated. Yes, it does take some healing to get to that point, but it is worth it, at least from what I have seen on my journey. Here's an example to illustrate this point: Let's say that you were raised Catholic but left it for various reasons. Then, twenty years later, a Catholic guide shows up out of the blue. If you left Catholicism on bad terms, then this may cause a knee-jerk emotional reaction, which is understandable. First, honor your emotions, and then secondly, ask yourself "why is this guide showing up now?" Next, pay attention to your life over the next couple of weeks. It could be that guide showed up because a Catholic idea will be coming up, and the guide wants you to be prepared for it. You may find that a theme or lesson over the next few weeks has to do with the Seven Deadly Sins, or the idea of Original Sin, or celibacy, or penance, or any combination of these, may come to the surface to be addressed, and therefore the guide is giving you a head's-up. You may not agree with any of these Catholic themes, and especially may not agree with them coming up in your life, but forewarned is forearmed, and with the guide's guidance, you are in a better position to respond. Or maybe the Catholic guide is not giving you a warning of what's coming up, but rather giving you a direction to look for your own development. In the above example, it could be that the guide is encouraging you to undertake a period of celibacy or is encouraging you to work with the idea of sacraments in your spiritual paradigm. I think this clarifies things, or at least I hope it does!

Third, who knows, really? The reasons an ancestral guide has for contacting us are as diverse as there are people on the planet so it is really hard to be comprehensive in our discussion. Just know though, that if some other reason becomes apparent that I have not discussed here, it would be wise to investigate that line of thought on your own. The rule of thumb is that if the guide is helping you grow and your life is showing positive, manifested results, then that is all that matters.

You can also pick up ancestor guides in some of the most bizarre ways. One time I was living in a place that was in the middle of three triangulated cemeteries.

Because of this, I would oftentimes get contacted by restless spirits from those places. Some would stay for a while, while others would just say hello and move on. The ones that tended to stay were ones that I had some sort of energetic or karmic connection with, such as being a Pisces, or being born and raised Catholic, or being left-handed! You can see that all of this meant that the connection between myself and them was not that strong, but it was still present and still had to be addressed. Another example of this is a time in my life when I was living in a particularly shady area of the city, and I would "pick-up" guides that died in the neighborhood. Usually these were just looking for someone to hear them and their stories, but sometimes they lingered longer when they discovered where I was at, spiritually and from an occult perspective. In this way they ended up being very strong, good guides, because they taught me about the neighborhood, and how to handle certain parts of the human psyche and that I had not been exposed to otherwise. There are more examples of this from my past, but I feel confident that these illustrate the point, so I see no reason to get into the rest of the stories here. These stories also highlight the transient nature of ancestral guide relationships. Even though the stories I just shared are not specifically ancestral guides, I do consider them ancestral guides, because they were path specific, and without them, I would probably not be where I am today, for better or for worse.

Exercise Seven: Continuing our exercises, now take some time to think about all of these points and consider who your ancestor guides are. If you are planning upcoming spiritual work, you may want to consider incorporating this material into your psyche ahead of time to maximize your gain. Record what you discover in your journal before proceeding.

Chapter Nine: Power Animal Guides

Like the previous chapter, this subject has been discussed in great depth and detail in many other volumes for a very long time. Working with animals, and the relationship that exists between humans and them, has been well documented in global cultures from various perspectives as long as the written word has existed, and naturally, over time, this extended to the spiritual world and relationships. There are many theories and thoughts behind why we have the animal companions we do. A lot of these vary from culture to culture, civilization to civilization.

This concept can be found in many places, ranging from holy books to philosophical texts. In many stories, a divine or semi-divine being has an encounter with an animal bearing a message from a Spirit, whether that message originated from a deity or not. One of the most glaring stories is of Horus from ancient Egyptian stories, who took the form of a hawk as well as a hawk headed God. While he did not bring messages to humanity from the spirit world as we are discussing here, he is one of the earlier examples of the integration of animals and humanity, even developing to the degree of blending animal and human traits. Another example of this is the dove so commonly found in Christian writings, where the dove was seen to be the bringer of peace, or at least the message of peace.

There is no real way to look at this concept from a historical context. The reason for this is that as long as humans have lived side by side with animals, there has been communication between the two, so this type of medicine goes back to the dawn of time, or at least as close as you can get. Other than petroglyphs, some of the earliest examples of the interplay between the species can be found in ancient Egypt, with their animal headed deities. The interplay between animals and humans has also been affected by different cultures that were influenced by their world views. For example, near the Mediterranean animals and interactions with them were regarded in a different way to those of the northern European region. In ancient Greek times animals were often identified as forces of nature that were meant to be, or were, controlled. However, in northern European areas animals were seen as powerful and wild. In the Native American tradition there was a certain harmony and coexistence that was present, rather than a conflicting perspective.

This subject got a boost in popularity in the 1960s with the occult renaissance that occurred in the western world due to the increased interest in Native American spirituality. Not only was the interest enhanced, there was also an explosion of printed material, both by indigenous people discussing their spirituality, and by those that were interested in the subject. Since then, more and more information has been shared, which has led to continual interest on the subject. Native American animal medicine wasn't the only way this information came to light. Backwoods American traditions also got brought into mass consciousness, and then of course, there was also the classical material of witches' familiars.

The Politically Correct Clarification

It's time to have a blunt conversation here, and while it is a tangent, it is important for establishing how ideas and conversations evolve, and have evolved, over time. With the modern information age around us, evolution is happening faster and faster, so you can be certain that parts of what I will discuss here will be outdated in the near future as well. Keep that in mind when you are reading this and adjust your understanding of this sensitive subject as you go through life. What I offer here is the establishment of a baseline.

When this interest was being developed in the 1960s, the main focus was on disseminating information. Accuracy, quite bluntly, was secondary. I realize this might be a surprise or even offensive to some people, but it is true, and here is the proof as to why. When I was learning about modern spirituality in the 1980s, the common phrase bandied about was "totem animal." It was a different time then, and this was acceptable, albeit inaccurate. If I learned this, then I am sure that millions of others learned this, too. The concept was simple: Each person has an animal in spirit form that they are connected with, that acts like a guide and companion as one progresses along their spiritual path. Sometimes this animal would be in physical form as well. You can see that the idea is spiritually sound, especially when you put this in context of the centuries-old tradition of the witch's familiar. From that perspective, we see that this is simply another term for a worldwide phenomenon.

Here is where the problem comes up. The word "totem," and associated ideas, such as "totem poles," are exclusively the provenance of Native American tribes in the Pacific Northwest part of the North American continent. So, for other tribes, such as the Cherokee that were located in other areas of the continent, they would not have used this term, but during the 1960s, 1970s, and even today, the use of this term continues. So, to clarify, to say that someone has a totem animal as a spirit guide would specifically refer to one of the indigenous tribes of that area of the continent, yet that is not the case today. The good news is that more and more people are using the term "power animal" as a replacement for this reason, and for reasons that have to do with the ongoing conversation of cultural appropriation. On one hand, this means that if material references "totem animals," it can probably still be relied on as useful for understanding animal symbolism, but on the other hand, you can only trust that information so far, because after all, they did not use the correct terms. In older books and writings this is highly forgivable, so there is that to consider, but this critical thinking should still be used when reviewing the material. As I get older, I get stricter about this point, intentionally ignoring material that came out under the term of "totem animal" or related titles, but that is just me. You do not have to be so stringent if you choose. I do suggest though, that you keep all of this in mind when you speak with Native Americans as a show of respect and an attempt at understanding. Sorry for the divergent here, but this is an important point, and one that is part of a developing conversation, so you may find things get clarified and delineated the further we move into the next century.

Instead of saying totem animal, using the term "power animal" is preferable. Sometimes you will find this subject referenced as "animal medicine," and personally that is my preference, because it is really more accurate. When you work with the energies of animals, you are working with them to enact your own healing. This is the medicinal role that they play. You can also think of the term "medicine" as similar to vitamins, rather than prescription drugs, as their roles in our lives may not be to heal something within us that is wrong, but rather to help us improve our overall health. I learned the term "animal medicine" from the Cherokee tradition, so if you look at other traditions, you may find variances, and if that happens, it is nothing to worry about.

Initial Points

Before we get into the details, there are a few general points to elucidate. The first one is that these relationships may have been formed in previous lives, and in this way, your power animal may be a spiritual companion that lasts a number of lives. There is also the possibility that in a previous lifetime the power animal was actually a physical animal rather than just a spiritual one. Yes, this means that the power animal in spirit that you have in this lifetime may have been a physical relationship in a previous life, and may again be a physical relationship in a future life.

In a lot of ways, considering this point illustrates the fact that energy recognizes energy, souls recognize souls. If you have ever had a strong familiarity when first meeting an animal, then you know the connection that I reference. Also keep in mind that just because an animal is one type of animal in this life, does not mean that it has always been the same animal, or even an animal at all. And, to make matters more complex, since we are discussing spirit animals here, it is worth pointing out that they may take the form of mythical creatures, such as basilisks, dragons, etc. Animals in spirit are not confined to the conservative interpretation and manifestation that we think they have, or should have. We are limited in physical ways, but if they are in spirit, then they are not. Many years ago I had a cat that I was closely connected with, and upon his transition, I got a message from a psychic that was quite profound. The psychic picked up on my grief, the type of animal he was, the color of his fur, but then also made the observation that he had not always been a cat when he and I had been together in previous lives. While I knew this to be true, I had also not shared that information with any other soul, living or dead. I also know that I might meet this cat's soul later in this lifetime again, or not, but if I do, he may not necessarily be a cat. While I am singling out one of my cats here, it is also true of another one, his sister, who was my familiar, and who has transitioned into spirit as well. I may meet up with both of them in this lifetime later, but they may not be cats, or I might not meet them in this lifetime again at all. Really, who knows? I don't sit around thinking about it, to be perfectly blunt, but from time to time I do ponder this interesting situation because ultimately I have no idea how it will play out. I will probably get to know them again, but whether they will be cats, or whether this will happen in this lifetime, I just, don't know.

A fine point to consider is one not discussed often, which is the fact that when you are dealing with a power animal, in spirit or not, you are dealing with an animal consciousness. This does not mean the animal is dumb in any way, but rather there are parameters to work within when dealing with them. This also means that one of the better things you can do to facilitate your relationship with them is to learn animal behavior. Yes, this does mean that you may spend a lot of time learning about a multitude of animals if you do a lot of work with them.

The Cheat Sheet

Following are principles to use when you are working with animal spirit guides. A seductive pitfall is to think that if a particular animal shows up, you should learn about that particular animal. The problem with this is that there is no way you can learn the symbolism of every animal that is out there, and to think that you can is a sign of hubris. Yes, I encourage you to research the animals that come up in your life, but before you go to all the trouble of researching them, you can learn a lot by knowing the following basic elements. I have found this information particularly useful when it comes to being put on the spot, and when having to make quick decisions and assessments. Feel free to adjust the following list of correspondences to your preference without losing the central essence of each element. Remember that we are dealing with an animal consciousness here, so K*I*S*S* (Keep It Simple, Silly!).

Land Animals

Usually the appearance of land animals signify addressing affairs of the physical world, and thus they are usually the most commonly noticed animals. For example, dogs correspond to loyalty, foxes to cunning, cats to playfulness, etc. Some of this can be deduced from knowing the behavior of animals, but often time subtleties take more discovery. For example, the skunk; skunk medicine corresponds to people giving you a wide birth out of respect, whereas some people may think there is a darker meaning to skunk medicine. It is also wise to pay attention to a sliding scale that is present here. There is a lot of difference between animals that live on the land, and animals that live under the land, such as an earthworm. It is always wise to keep this in mind. Generally, animals that live under the earth have to do with burrowing down deep on a subject. However, it can also mean going deep down to fortify the self or finding the treasures of the underworld.

Part of the analysis of earth animal medicine also has to do with environment in several ways. If you're getting messages from an animal that is not indigenous to your area, you may find that part of the message has to do with exploring that environment for personal growth because what it is and/or what it represents may be particularly useful at this time in your life. However, if you receive messages from animals that are indigenous to your area, this is also a message that is saying to be where you are at the moment. These are often animals that are associated with *doing* something rather than reading something or emoting something. When one works with the physical earth, whether it's gardening or getting the next business project done, one tunes into the practical and the manifested.

Finally, some good old fashioned common sense should

be applied. Let's look at chickens for example. Chickens don't fly the same way that birds do, even though they have wings. Hence they would correspond to earth rather than air, which we will talk about shortly. Another example of this is temperature. If an animal does well at high temperatures then it would be wise to keep this in mind, as it can reveal to you what to expect in the near future as the next step on your path. This can easily be worked with if you know the correspondences of the four basic elements of the western tradition: earth, air, fire, and water. The final element, spirit, we'll talk about in a little bit.

Water Animals

If aqua-animals are showing up, then it is time to work with the emotions in some form. This also includes working with the intuition and the psychic side of life. Compassion, love, and all related concepts also come under the sway of this category, and thus these animals can sometimes take finesse to work with rather than the brute like strength that may be required with land animals.

Another point to consider that is similar to what was mentioned above is that it is wise to pay attention to how deep in the water the animal is. This could have a similar connotation to what was mentioned above. For example, an animal that swims deeper underwater than another may be telling you to go deep within yourself and your emotions to get to the root of whatever situation it is that's going on. However, an extension of this is that it is wise to pay attention to animals that feed off of the bottom, commonly called "bottom feeders." The reason for this is that often those represent conditions and situations that have to do with taking in the forgotten or the lowest kind of vibrational energy that is out there, rather than being fully integrated into things. This can be seen as a parallel to carrion energy, feeding off of the dead rather than the living.

Amphibians are also worth noting, as they reveal something special to us. Amphibious animals are those that can easily navigate land and water, and thus their appearance has to do with adaptability and the grace that is required to work with the two worlds so that they are harmonized. Discussing amphibians opens the door to a deeper conversation, which is that of hybrid environment animals. Amphibians are the clearest examples of this, but there are other paradoxes of the animal world to consider. Let's turn our attention back to the valued chicken. Yes, it is a bird, so you would want to look at bird correspondences, but it is a bird that does not fly. It glides, but it does not fly, so while traditional bird correspondences would apply, they would be tempered by this fact. The colors of animals would also be wise to note. Colors have traits associated to them, and when you are analyzing animal medicine, it is smart to put this into perspective of your analysis, too.

The same concept mentioned above having to do with local or exotic environments also comes into play here. If you are landlocked and you have a visit from a sea animal, then perhaps it's time to take a trip to the ocean. However, it may also simply be a good time to expand your emotions and working with emotions to encompass a bigger world view. In this particular example it is also wise to pay attention to salt water vs. freshwater. In esotericism, salt is a cleansing agent, and thus part of the message may be that it is time to do some emotional cleansing.

These are the animals that are representative of the *feeling* side of existence rather than the *doing* side, which corresponds to land animals. Because of this, their appearances may often have to do with us putting ourselves in a state of emotional vulnerability while we process and work through our situations. Trusting our feelings and developing our intuition and psychic side are two concepts that are usually being called for when this medicine appears. For some this may be challenging because its foreign, but in other ways this may be challenging because it can be too much of a good thing.

Air Animals

Animals that fly on the winds of the air tend to be animals that address the mental body, psychology, and spirituality. Usually when we get messages from these animals they are telling us things that have to do with internal work within ourselves, and they address ideas that we can comprehend using our minds and our spirits. Thus, they may have to do with taking up new subjects, embracing new philosophies, and also rising to the mental plane to overcome other issues. The same thing that was mentioned above about exotic or familiar environments should also be considered here.

These are the animals that are representative of thinking, rather than feeling or doing, and they are a reminder of our own inherent ability to rise above it all through the power of the mind. However, these animals often feed from either the water or the land, so they serve as a reminder that no matter how cerebral we get, we will still have to come down to the emotional and/or the physical in order to get sustenance. We may cultivate the ability to rise above it all, but we never freely fly above the land or water until we drop our physical form.

While true of all animals, it is a particularly wise decision to contemplate the colors that are adorned by animals of the air. Often birds are known for their vibrant colors, and colors are worth paying attention to when analyzing bird medicine. Another related topic is that of a bird's song, pay attention to whether or not a bird has a song it is known for. Songs can be analyzed in a number of different ways, in particular that some of the most beautiful sounds come from songbirds.

"Mythological" Animals

We may also get messages from animals that aren't "real," or at least that is what some people will say about them. For example, the phoenix. This does not mean that we should ignore the messages from them, but rather it would be wise to look in different places for this information. Throughout the western tradition, amalgamations of animals have been used to convey different esoteric thoughts and concepts. The biggest body of study that addresses this is alchemy, so it is wise to start there. Usually these animals are made up of other, more common animals, so therefore if we break them down into their component beasts, we can better understand what they are trying to tell us.

Many times, these mythological creatures veil astrological truths in addition to occultism teachings, so you can uncover a lot of their hidden messages by learning astrology. While this is a conversation for another time and place, it is worth pointing out here for the sake of completeness. Sometimes this even includes astronomical events, such as eclipses, so their messages are not just relegated to occultism. If you recall what we discussed earlier about the connection between alchemy and chemistry, you can see that many times these animals will show up when working with the Doctor of Chemistry Guide and related situations. This is of course not one hundred percent true, but it is a good rule of thumb to follow when and if they show up in your life.

Exercise Eight: Using the Spirit Guide Contact Ritual Template from chapter two, make contact with one or several of your power animals, and record the results in your journal. You can do this in a very relaxed way, such as being content making content with one spirit animal, or you could make this more stringent by attempting to make contact with one spirit animal from each element. It really doesn't matter, but in time, you may find you gravitate to the latter.

Chapter Ten: Final Points and Cautions

There is very little ground left to cover in this book, yet there is still so much ground left to cover when it comes to your spiritual journey. Here, I have given you the map, but most assuredly it is not the territory. As you develop your relationships with your guides, you will uncover many things not addressed here. But, as this happens, you may also find that the principles discussed here are still prevalent, and in that way, it is my intention that this book will continue to give you value as you grow through life. As we cultivate our spirit associate relationships, we put ourselves in a position to better understand the deeper mysteries of the multiverse.

Many different methods exist for making guide contact, and here I have only covered a few. Meditation, ritual, and channeling, are the three dominant preferred techniques used by most people, but there are other methods that can be used, such as ecstatic trance. As long as a technique is wholesome, I encourage you to explore it, but there are some words of warning that should be shared.

First, as briefly discussed earlier, it is wise to avoid being overly reliant on your guides. If you constantly ask them to make decisions for you, for whatever reason, then you are staring at a red flag. Whether you do this to avoid personal responsibility and accountability, or to become closer to them (or so you tell yourself), this is still not a wise course of action to undertake. Relying on them too much is a bad thing, as is true with all relationships in life. Spirit associates are here to help us, not to do things for us. They are meant as guides and allies, that's all, and like most guides, their roles in our life should be minimized to a certain degree. From another perspective, it is wise to remember that they have things to do on the other side of the veil as well. We are not their only relationships, and since time flows differently over there, we are not in a good position to relate to them in a linear sense. Codependency is something that can occur across the veil and is not limited to just human to human interactions.

Secondly, make sure to stay grounded in the physical world when you are doing guide work. I have known many people over the years that have let their lives go because they were so into working with their spirit associates, predominantly guides. This is spiritual escapism and is toxic and a form of denial. A good rule of thumb for spiritual development across the boards is that it should be a form of enhancement for life, rather than a form of escapism *from* life. This is a point that has been discussed in a lot of modern spirituality writings, but I will hit key points here, and I encourage you to dig deeper if you are interested in this topic. When you decide to work with your spirit guides, it should be from a space of empowerment, not desperation. This also tiptoes into the realm of verified personal gnosis and unverified personal gnosis that we have previously discussed. Many times people establish a connection with their guides and receive what they believe to be profound insight. This leads to a desire for more information and a deeper connection. If left unchecked, this can turn into an obsession. This obsession can then lead to mental instability and a host of other psychological issues. Delusions of grandeur is also a danger that can come from this behavior, and this is one of the more insidious manifestations because everyone is looking for something to make them special in the eyes of the world, and in their own eyes. You can see how the more psychologically damaged a person is, the more of a temptation this can be.

Third, which is a common problem in many spiritual circles, is that it is far too easy to read about spirit guides and associates, but never do the work. The quantity of information collected about spirit relationships never makes up for the quality of information gleaned through meditation and other approaches. This gets a lot of attention in occultism, and there it is known as being an "armchair magician." This refers to someone that does a lot of reading and study, but never does the work. Again, like the previous point, this is a behavior that is very seductive, but ultimately detracts from spiritual and personal development. Yes, it is wise to be well-read about the subject, and I encourage you to do so, but ultimately, if you don't put this information to work for you, then you really aren't executing spiritual growth. Instead, you are simply being a fan, rather than a participant. There is nothing wrong with being a fan of something, but if this is the case, then one should admit it to themselves and to others.

This opens the door to point four, which is that of humility. A working premise of this book is that everyone has these spirit guides around them, and while not everyone will make contact with all of them like we are discussing here, many will make contact with at least their Master Teacher guide. It is important to know this because it means that while it may feel special to make a connection with spirit guides, it really isn't that special in the grand scheme of things. In "Spirit Relations," I discuss the fact that everyone is born psychic, but not everyone has the same strengths in the same areas, or in the same ways. "Pride cometh before a fall," as the common saying goes, and it is easy to become arrogant through spirit work. One of the ways to stay humble is to remember that many times people are working with their guides in unknowing ways. I have seen that many people work with their guides in a subconscious way, not realizing that they are, in fact, working with guides at all. On many occasions this plays out as previously discussed; listening to the voice in one's head, or feeling like they are being guided by an unseen entity during important times of their lives. I have even seen that sometimes, people that have an unknowing connection with their guides have a better relationship with them, than someone that has a knowing relationship. Humility is something that is an important spiritual trait in general, and this is especially true here. The opposite of this though, is that you do not want to have so much humility that you lack self-confidence. Self-confidence should be increased through guide work.

Along that line of thought, it is also worth noting that another danger present is that of thinking you need the approval of your spirit associates. They are here to help us, not approve or disapprove of our actions. Another common behavioral pattern I have seen over the decades is that someone makes a choice whether to do something or not based on whether they think their spirit guide(s) will approve of their actions. Bluntly, spirit allies don't care. Yes, they want to see us succeed, and thus they have a vested interest, but they also know that we are incarnated in a free will zone, so the choices are ultimately ours. They, too, have free will, and even though they are subjected to the laws of karma, they also have the freedom to assess what they are doing and why, and to make changes in their behavior accordingly. After all, if they see that they are putting more work into the relationship than they are getting out of it, it is actually healthy for them to leave the relationship. Spirit associates do not sit in judgment of us and our actions. Really, technically, there is no spiritual being that sits in judgment of us. I realize that some religions do not share this view, so I will one hundred percent admit the subjectivity of my line of thought here, but this view is based on logic. Most religions have at their essence, a message of love, and love is not judgmental if it is true. Therefore, the only judgment we bring with us on our spiritual path is that which we have created in our minds from various programming instances in our past. When someone spiritually unfolds, a subconscious tendency is to transfer previous spiritual beliefs onto the newly found spiritual path. Not only does this pollute and dilute the new teachings, it is also simply a transference of baggage from one paradigm to another, and shows a lack of understanding and growth. The saving grace here though, is that many people do this unconsciously, so they cannot be held accountable for this if they do not know any better. How does someone respond when this is pointed out to them? That is the true determining factor of humility and growth. If someone has this pointed out to them, how do they react? If they react with a sincere desire to understand and correct this, then you can be assured that they are serious about their spiritual growth. If they disagree with the person that points this out, then that makes its own statement, too.

This is a point that I have seen a lot in the "New Age" scene over the last twenty years or so, and bluntly, I had to work through this too, and like so many others, I was guilty of doing this subconsciously because I didn't know any better. Here are a couple of examples to illustrate the point. Let's say that you were born and raised Christian, but then you discover and start working with Thelema, which has the Egyptian god Horus as a central figure. It would be too easy to seek the approval of Horus, much like many Christians seek the approval of their god. Another, more generic example, would be in thinking that morality is an inherent trait of the spirit world. If you stop and think about this for a few moments, you should see other examples of this committed by people. The easy way to prevent this is to be aware of it, and then to do your research whenever you are transitioning from one spiritual paradigm to another. This does mean you will encounter deeply held beliefs, and re-evaluating them might be initially painful, but in the long run, this is one of the healthiest things you can do for your spirit. To truly be liberated of a previous spiritual paradigm means to be able to look at it analytically, extract the pearls of wisdom from it, and be empowered enough to know when to work with those teachings, and when to work with your new, chosen, spiritual paradigm. Be warned though, that one of the things that makes this complex are the number of parallels that exist between various religions. Parallels between Confucianism and Buddhism come to mind, as well as Christianity and Islam. This makes it sometimes difficult to differentiate parallel teachings from similar religions, so it is very understandable that working with this idea will take some time and energy, and may include periodic backslides, so being compassionate with yourself is wise to do as you go through this transitory process.

Point six on our list of cautions is that of a lack of trust. This is slightly complex and specific, but it does require some explanation. If you say that you believe in and work with spirit guides, but then never trust them when they give you insight and direction and follow their lead, then you really aren't maximizing your gain or living your talk. This does mean you will routinely be taken out of your comfort zone, and that is a large part of the point of this. While this is true on average, it should also be tempered with common sense. Blind trust should never be put into your guides. For example, if one of your spirit guides says it would be wise for you to move across the country, you should immediately question that information, especially if you just got settled in where you are currently living. True, uplifting spiritual relationships with authentic, spiritual beings, will never put you in a position like that. You can use this line of thinking as a tool for critical thinking as you spiritually develop through life. Yes, you should trust your guides, but no, you should not *blindly* trust them. As we discussed previously, when you set up password-like protocols with your guides, you all but eliminate this possibility. It would be wise to make sure you don't get lulled into a false sense of security when working with them to the degree that you skip those established protocols, even if you think your intuition is telling you this is okay.

I will share a story from my own life to illustrate the complexities of this point. Up until the last year or so, I did a LOT of work with spirits of various pantheons, paradigms, and types. When you do a lot of spirit work like this, a fundamental practice is to always test your spirits. I did not do this initially when I started working with my spirit guides, even though I did it with other spirits I encountered. One day during meditation it occurred to me that to truly live a life of divine alignment and integrity, I should be testing my spirit guides as well. Since these relationships were already established, I did not feel it necessary to test them as frequently as I tested other spirits. Part of the reason for this is because I do regular banishings to keep my space clean. Another part of the reason is because spirit guides are a finer type of spirit than what most people encounter when doing heavy occultism work. So, instead of testing them during every interaction, I decided to test them once a year, as a sort of annual checkup. This worked for me for several years, but I noticed that over time, my guides became less responsive to my tests. Eventually, they quit passing the tests entirely, and at the time, I interpreted this to mean that they were exposed as frauds. During this period, I was routinely doing my regular banishings as well, so I knew that the changes were not brought about through any deficiency on my part. Because they quit responding, I quit working with them. Why work with spirits that cannot or will not justify or validate their existence?

During that time I was in touch with many other like-minded individuals, and they thought I was a little more stringent than they would be, but they understood my perspective. After I stopped working with them, I spent time in meditation on the subject because I wanted to make sure that I was, in fact, not in the wrong. It was during this time that I remembered that they are subjected to the laws of karma just like I am, and because of this, their choice to not honor our connection is something they will deal with later, which means all of us (them and myself) will probably have a sit-down discussion in the spirit world after I am dead, and during that, we will get all of this sorted out. However, I would rather work with spirit guides on a regular basis now while I'm alive. This all happened several years ago, and since then, I have resolved this spiritual situation, but it did take a few years to straighten things out.

Take all of the lessons from this that you can extract, and apply them to your spiritual journey, but I will share a few here that I took from this chapter of my spiritual life. First, always test your spirits! I knew that ahead of time, but this was a strong reminder. Secondly, if you do decide to take this route, figure out a regular testing pattern. If you test them too often, that might imply that you do not trust them, which is damaging and detrimental to the relationship. But, if you do not test them often enough, then you put yourself in a position where the connection can fade or be manipulated. Your only saving grace with this point is to keep up on your daily cleansings and banishings. Third, this served as a reminder to me that they are subjected to the laws of karma just like I am. Fourth, if spirits, guides or not, take issue with you testing them, then you deserve better spirits to guide you. Fifth, if you take approaches like this when it comes to your spirit guides, you may find that you meet with backlash from people you know, because this is not a traditional part of Spiritualism or spirit guide work. Luckily, I did not meet with that kind of backlash, but I could easily see how that might happen to someone. Sixth, this drove home the point of doing your daily cleansings. After all, if I had not been doing that, then I could not test my spirits with a clear conscience, and I would not have been as objective as I was. Seventh, just because the nature of the relationship between you and your spirit associates is intimate, does not give you an excuse to not treat them like other spirits you might work with, if any. As you can see from this story, I did my best to apply compassion and this understanding to the situation by only testing them once a year, rather than once every interaction, but if you decide you want to test them every eighteen months instead, or some other pattern that is more appropriate for you, then feel free. I offer the above story simply as an illustration to inspire your practice. Eighth, spirit associates do not like to be tested. I could feel the resistance from them every year when I executed the test. To this day, I still do not understand why that was the case, but it was, none the less. Yes, relationships built on love should, in a perfect world, be "test-free," and in my paradigm, that is definitely the case for physical relationships built on love. When we're talking about relationships with spirits though, things get a little more complex. When dealing with spirit associates, they should be approached from a space of love, but as I quoted previously, "Trust in Allah, but tie up your camel."

Because our vision in the spirit world is not as sharp or as developed as our physical sight, we will never see what they see, and they will never see what we see. This also means that part of the responsibility falls on our shoulders, to keep our energy clear on a daily basis. By doing this, we show our love for them and our spiritual progress. There are more lessons I could share here, but I think the above eight make my point. If you work with some of this material, then you will acquire your own lessons, which may or may not be some of the ones I shared. In any event, consider this personal experience an insight into operative spiritual work.

You can see how this story highlights the fine balance of trust to cultivate with your spirit guides. Yes, trust them, but do not trust them that much. Then again, this could be applied to many relationships in life, so embracing this perspective is something that is more natural than not. It is simply uncomfortable for most people since we are discussing something so intimate and personal.

Caution point seven is to remember that joy is a higher vibrational energy than most other emotions, which means that when you are dealing with them, don't take yourself too seriously, and don't take your work with them too seriously. Have fun and have fun with them! Life is too short to be constantly serious with them. The converse is also noteworthy though, which is that if your only interactions with them are playful and joyous, then they can't really take you seriously, either, which could be counterproductive.

Point eight is a controversial but important one. When we work with various guides and associates in spirit, we are connecting with beings that we want to be like-minded with us. This means that if we are not careful, we are creating an echo chamber. I know some of you might not be familiar with this concept, so a brief digression is necessary for clarification. An echo chamber is a common phrase for the notion that one surrounds themselves only with people that share their views and allows no room for different perspectives or opinions. Effectively, the only information shared in the echo chamber are echoes of one's views. While this is good for validation, and good on a metaphysical level, it can be bad because this sort of closed-circuit behavior can stagnate growth, create fascist behavior and thought, and can even be an indoctrination to cult thinking of a sort.

Spirit guides are just that, guides. When we communicate with them, we are looking for deeper insights and further information to help us on our spiritual path. This means that most of the time our guides will be giving us information that is in line with who we are, what we know, and where we *think* we are going, spiritually speaking. This can lead one to relax their thought processes, and only listen to information that coincides with preconceived notions. The sign of a good teacher is telling you where to look, but not telling you what you will find, and this is especially true of guides. What this means is that if you have an open mind when communicating with your guides, you will find they will subtly cause you to look at things in a new light and from a new perspective. They will not necessarily say that you're wrong, but rather they will phrase their wisdom in such a way to encourage you to arrive at that conclusion on your own. Sometimes your guides will bluntly tell you that you are wrong on somethings, but this is based on how you are as a person. If you are a direct person like that, then yes, they may use that approach with you, but if you are not a direct kind of person, then they will not be direct with you. There have been many times in my life when my guides have encouraged me to look in different directions than I would have if left to my own devices, and this usually happened in gentle ways. Other times though, I have received direct "noes" from them as well, so their approach to you may vary from time to time.

If you keep these in mind when you are deepening your relationships with your spirit associates, you put yourself in a position of empowerment, not just for your work with them, but also for greater success in the manifested world. There are other cautions that are more specific to you and your spiritual path, so while this list is fairly comprehensive, it is not definitive. I encourage you to add and subtract points to this as you grow from here.

Appendix A: Reference List

This is a recap of exercises and other useful tidbits from the rest of the text. It is intended to be a one-stop reference for those that desire a shortcut. Chapter references will be included for your use.

-Preparation for spirit work-chapter two.

-Sacred space creation-chapter two.

-Spirit guide contact template-chapter two.

-Exercise One-Assess the nature of the relationship, if any, that you have with your spirit guide or guides.

-Exercise Two-Recall your childhood friend, if it can be recalled-chapter three.

-Exercise Three-Contact your gatekeeper guide-chapter four.

-Exercise Four-Contact your Doctor of Philosophy guide-chapter five.

-Exercise Five-Contact your Doctor of Chemistry guide-chapter six.

-Exercise Six-Discover and list your secondary and specialty guides-chapter seven.

-Exercise Seven-Discover and connect with your ancestor guides-chapter eight.

-Exercise Eight-Contact your power animal guide-chapter nine.

Bibliography/For Further Reading

https://www.psychologytoday.com/us/blog/the-human-experience/200904/personal-power, taken from "The Ethics of Interpersonal Relationships," 2009.

Animal Spirit Guides by Steven Farmer

Ask Your Guides by Sonia Choquette

Buckland's Book of Spirit Communication.

How to Meet and Work with Spirit Guides by Ted Andrews

Power Animals by Steven Farmer

Spirit Allies by Christopher Penczak

Sacred Contracts by Caroline Myss

Spirit Guides and Angel Guardians by Richard Webster.

Spirit Relations by Bill Duvendack

Talking to the Dead by Barbara Weisberg

The Astral Plane by C.W. Leadbeater

The Heyday of Spiritualism by Slater Brown

The History of Spiritualism by Sir Arthur Conan Doyle

The Mighty Dead by Christopher Penczak

The Psychic Mafia, by M Lamar Keene

Working with your Guides and Angels by Ruth White

Working with Spirit Guides by Ruth White

Recent Titles from Megalithica Books

The Elemental Magic Workbook 2nd Edition by Soror Velchanes

This pragmatic workbook offers a complete course in elemental magic and provides a solid foundation for future independent work. Throughout history, individuals from diverse backgrounds and preparations have harnessed the elemental forces for spiritual enrichment, life balance, practical magic, and more. Though many cultures developed similar (and also valuable) models, our primary emphasis will be on understanding and working with the elements from ancient Greek and Hermetic perspectives, with a chaos magic twist. ISBN: 978-1-912241-18-7 Price: £11.99, $17.50

SHE: Primal Meetings with the Dark Goddess by Storm Constantine & Andrew Collins

The Dark Goddess is unpredictable, dispassionate, cruel, and often deadly. She reflects our deepest desires, fears, hopes and expectations. In this fully-illustrated book, Storm Constantine and Andrew Collins have selected a fascinating range of 34 goddesses, including some who are not so well-known. The pathworkings to meet them and explore their realms will offer insight into these often-misunderstood deities. (This title is also available as a limited edition, numbered hardback.) ISBN: 978-1-912241-06-4 Price: £12.99, $18.99

Quantum Sorcery 3rd Edition by Dave Smith

Quantum Sorcery is a modern magical system through which an individual can learn to manifest desired effects in the physical world through the exertion of Will, assisted by appropriate symbols and tools. This paradigm incorporates elements from earlier magical systems as well as physics, psychology, mathematics and biology to propose a mechanism by which such an act might occur through means more natural than supernatural.

ISBN: 978-1-912241-19-4 Price: £11.99, $17.50

www.immanion-press.com

www.ingramcontent.com/pod-product-compliance
Lightning Source LLC
LaVergne TN
LVHW051002080826
845145LV00009B/2412

* 9 7 8 1 9 1 2 2 4 1 2 0 0 *